The Passion of Jesus in the Gospel of John

The Passion Series

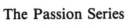

Volume 4

The Passion of Jesus in the Gospel of John

by
Donald Senior, C.P.

A Michael Glazier Book
THE LITURGICAL PRESS
Collegeville, Minnesota

Cover design by Lillian Brulc.

2   3   4   5   6   7   8   9

Library of Congress Cataloging-in-Publication Data

Senior, Donald.
    The passion of Jesus in the Gospel of John / by Donald Senior.
        p.   cm. — (The Passion series ; v. 4)
    "A Michael Glazier book."
    Includes bibliographical references and index.
    ISBN 0-8146-5462-2
    1. Jesus Christ—Passion. 2. Bible. N.T. John—Criticism,
interpretation, etc. I. Title. II. Series: Senior, Donald.
Passion series ; v. 4.
BT431.S449 1991   91-12961
226.5'06—dc20   CIP

CONTENTS

PREFACE

With this volume on John, the Passion series concludes its study of the meaning of Jesus' death in each of the Gospels.[1] Even though it comes fourth in the sequence, John's Gospel is by no means a repetition of what went before. In its portrayal of the death of Jesus, as in every other aspect of its message, John's Gospel is distinctive and unique. It earns its title as a "maverick" Gospel.[2]

As is well known and often commented on, John portrays Jesus in exalted, luminous tones. Jesus speaks in long meditative discourses whose focus is usually on his own identity as the unique revealer of God and the way to salvation. Jesus' claims to be the "Son of God" (5:17-18), to exist prior to Abraham (8:58) are matched by the Gospel's description of him as the eternal Word who springs forth from God and returns to God (1:1; 13:1). Thomas' acclamation at the end of the narrative—"My Lord and My God" (20:28)—hardly catches the reader by surprise.

But at the same time, John portrays Jesus in emphatically earthy tones: The Word becomes "flesh" (1:14) and that "flesh" is given for the life of the world (6:51). The one who believes in Jesus is to "eat" his flesh and "drink" his blood (6:53). While the Johannine Jesus at times may seem to tread lightly on the surface of this world, John is attentive to the physical contours of that

[1] See D. Senior, *The Passion of Jesus in the Gospel of Matthew* (Passion Series 1; Wilmington: Michael Glazier, 1985); *The Passion of Jesus in the Gospel of Mark* (Passion Series 2; Wilmington: Michael Glazier, 1984); *The Passion of Jesus in the Gospel of Luke* (Passion Series 3; Wilmington: Michael Glazier, 1989).

[2] The name is applied by R. Kysar in his introduction to John's Gospel, *John, The Maverick Gospel* (Atlanta: John Knox, 1976).

land and the city of Jerusalem, revealing a more accurate knowledge of the city and the country than the Synoptics do.[3]

Much of what is distinctive about John's portrayal of Jesus
comes from the evangelist's ability to mix symbol and narrative,
to play upon paradox and irony, to suffuse historical description
with exalted theological interpretation—all in the service of his
vision of the Gospel. That "vision" has a penetrating, intuitive
quality to it. John's Gospel has a "contemplative" atmosphere,
riveting its attention on the essential truth of the Gospel: Jesus
is the Word of God who comes into the world to reveal God's
overwhelming love for the world. The more complex and multiple features of the Synoptic tradition seem to dissolve and merge
in John's theology. Now the focus is on Jesus and his transcendent identity. All struggles forge into one ultimate struggle: the
struggle between life and death, between love and hatred, between
light and darkness. The demands of discipleship are reduced to
belief in Jesus and imitation of his selfless love. The humanity
of Jesus is not suppressed in John but takes on a luminous quality; in and through the "flesh" of Jesus God is revealed to the
world.

The triumph of Jesus over the power of death is nowhere more
apparent than in the Passion narrative of John's Gospel. But at
the same time, John, much more overtly than the Synoptic
Gospels, does not overlook the physical aspects of Jesus' suffering and death: he is slapped in the face; must carry his own cross
to execution; cries out in thirst; and to confirm his death a lance
is thrust through his side and draws out blood and water. Precisely through the sufferings and death of Jesus—realities which
certify his humanness, his being "flesh"—God's love for the
world is enacted and proclaimed.

The Passion is, in fact, the summit of John's Gospel and the
ultimate expression of its message. To understand the meaning
of Jesus' death is to comprehend the powerful revelation that
drives this Gospel from start to finish. And throughout Christian history, believers have drawn inspiration and comfort from

---

[3] For example, John's Gospel is aware of such Jerusalem features as the pool of the Beth-
szatha near the Sheep Gate where healing took place (5:2); the pool of Siloam (9:7); and
the precise location of Gethsamene ("across the winter-flowing 'Kidron' wadi" 18:1).

John's Passion because of its bold proclamation of love's triumph over death. Images of "coming home" to the "many mansions" of the Father's house, of "returning to God," of "completing the work God gave one to do," of "laying down one's life for one's friend," of death as moment of "glory" rather than defeat are all Johannine images which have a deep hold on Christian consciousness. John's Passion narrative is proclaimed every Good Friday to all the Church, boring into the memory of the Church at one of the most gripping moments in its liturgical year.

The amount of scholarship devoted to John's Gospel in the past few years has been staggering.[4] The attraction of this Gospel, its enticing complexity, and the resulting debates over its interpretation, have driven modern day scholars to produce massive and even multi-volumed commentaries.[5] Surprisingly, however, few books have been devoted exclusively to John's Passion narrative.[6] Our goal in this study is to focus on that key dimension of the Gospel. Through a study of Jesus' Passion in John's Gospel one has the opportunity to probe the heart of his entire Gospel message.

Studying John's account does pose some special challenges. One area of debate is the issue of what sources the evangelist drew upon in fashioning his Passion narrative. While there is a strong

---

[4] Confer the survey of R. Kysar, *The Fourth Evangelist and His Gospel: An Examination of Contemporary Scholarship* (Minneapolis: Augsburg, 1975) and the earlier bibliographical summary of E. Malatesta, *St. John's Gospel: 1920–1965: A Cumulative and Classified Bibliography of Books and Periodical Literature on the Fourth Gospel* (Analecta Biblica 32; Rome: Biblical Institute Press, 1967), and the follow-up to this in G. Van Belle, *Johannine Bibliography 1966–1985. A Cumulative Bibliogrpahy on the Fourth Gospel* (Leuven: Leuven University Press, 1988).

[5] See, for example, the two volumes of R. Brown, *The Gospel According to John I-XII* (AB 29; Garden City: Doubleday, 1966); *The Gospel According to John XIII-XXI* (AB 29A; Doubleday, 1970), the three volumes of R. Schnackenburg, *The Gospel According to St. John* (New York: Seabury, 1980–83), and such massive single volume works as C.K. Barrett, *The Gospel According to St. John* (Philadelphia: Westminster, 2nd ed., 1978), B. Lindars, *The Gospel of John* (New Century Bible; Greenwood, SC: Attic Press, 1977), and G. Beasley-Murray, *John* (Word Biblical Commentary 36; Waco: Word, 1987), to name a very few.

[6] See, for example, A. Dauer, *Die Passionsgeschichte im Johannesevangelium* (STANT 30; München: Kösel, 1972); J. Bligh, *The Sign of the Cross* (Sough: St. Paul Publications, 1975); I. De la Potterie, *The Hour of Jesus* (Staten Island: Alba House, 1989); J. T. Forestell, *The Word of the Cross. Salvation as Revelation in the Fourth Gospel* (Analecta Biblica 57; Rome: Biblical Institute Press, 1974). Articles on specific scenes or aspects of John's Passion are numerous.

consensus that Matthew and Luke in some fashion depended on Mark as the primary source of their narratives, there is much less consensus in John's case.[7] It is clear that John's Passion narrative, from the moment of Jesus' arrest through to his death and burial (chapters 18 and 19), has stronger parallels to the Synoptic accounts than in any other major section of his Gospel, leading some exegetes to conclude that John's account is a creative interpretation of the Synoptic tradition. But John's narrative remains distinct in so many respects that many scholars doubt there was any direct contact between the Johannine author and the Synoptic versions. The similarities between John and the Synoptics would result from that fact that both John and Mark, independently of each other, drew on an older and fairly fixed tradition concerning the death of Jesus.[8]

The issue of the sources for John's Gospel as a whole is a much wider and even more tangled debate. Some modern interpreters have suggested that John drew on a "Signs" source to construct the major part of his portrayal of Jesus' public ministry in chapters 1–12. This source would have concentrated on Jesus' great miracles or "signs" and presented Jesus as a messianic wonder-worker. At a later stage, the Johannine evangelist would have blended in with this "Signs" source, the narrative of Jesus' death and resurrection, appended the prologue to the opening of the Gospel, and suffused the entire narrative with his exalted christology—eventually giving the Gospel its present basic shape and character.[9]

Speculation about the major sources of the Gospel is also joined to debate about the stages of the Gospel's construction. Recent scholarship has attempted to chart the evolution of the Johan-

---

[7] See the succinct history and discussion of this issue in D. Moody Smith, *John* (Proclamation Commentaries; Philadelphia: Fortress, rev. ed., 1986), pp. 2–11, who concludes that a direct relationship to the Synoptic Gospels is doubtful and, in any case, not decisive for interpretation of the Gospel; the direct dependence of John on Mark's Gospel is vigorously upheld by F. Neirynck, *Jean et les Synoptiques* (BETL 49; Leuven: Leuven University Press, 1979).

[8] See the thesis elaborated in J. Green, *The Death of Jesus* (WUNT 33; Tübingen: J.C.B. Mohr, 1988).

[9] See R. T. Fortna, *The Fourth Gospel and Its Predecessor* (Philadelphia: Fortress, 1988); and U. C. von Wahlde, *The Earliest Version of John's Gospel, Recovering the Gospel of Signs* (Wilmington: Michael Glazier, 1989).

nine community itself and the resulting impact on the formation of the Gospel.[10] The Christian community that stands behind the Gospel had its roots in Palestinian Judaism but may also have been influenced at an early stage of its history by an influx of Samaritan converts and, ultimately, Gentile Christians. Some scholars believe that the first disciples who formed the nucleus of the Johannine community may have come from "heterodox" Judaism, that is, from groups who stood more on the fringe of Jewish religious life at the time of Jesus and the early decades of the Christian movement. This plus the influx of Samaritans and later Gentile converts would contribute to the more "maverick" character of this Gospel which stands apart from the more "mainline" traditions evident in the Synoptic Gospel. Some speculate that at a certain point, the community would have moved out of a Palestinian context all together and into the Gentile world, either in Ephesus or some other center. John's Gospel, therefore, would bear the influence of both Hellenistic and specifically Jewish patterns of thought.[11]

It is also clear that John's community stood in some sharp tension with Pharisaic Judaism. The controversy between Jesus and the Pharisees in chapter 9 of the Gospel, with the threat to eject from the Synagogue the man born blind and his parents because of belief in Jesus, may reflect the controversies between rabbinic Judaism and early Christianity that developed in the period after the destruction of the Temple in A.D. 70[12] As we will discuss below, this experience of the Johannine community may have had a direct influence on the negative way the Evangelist portrays the opponents of Jesus.[13]

---

[10] See, for example, J. L. Martyn, *History and Theology in the Fourth Gospel* (Nashville: Abingdon, 2nd rev. ed., 1979); R. Brown, *The Community of the Beloved Disciple* (New York: Paulist, 1979); and the earlier works of C. K. Barrett, *The Gospel of John & Judaism* (Philadelphia: Fortress, 1975); O. Cullmann, *The Johannine Circle* (Philadelphia: Westminster, 1975). For a survey of the issue, see John Ashton (ed.), *The Interpretation of John* (Issues in Religion and Theology 9; Philadelphia: Fortress, 1986), pp. 1-17.

[11] See D. Senior & C. Stuhlmueller, *The Biblical Foundations for Mission* (Maryknoll: Orbis, 1983), 280-83; G. MacRae, "The Fourth Gospel and *Religionsgeschichte,*" *Catholic Biblical Quarterly* 32 (1970), 13-24.

[12] This is the major thesis of J. L. Martyn, *History & Theology in the Fourth Gospel;* see also, R. Brown, *Community of the Beloved Disciple,* 40-43.

[13] See below, Part I, pp. 39-42.

The possibility of various sources blended into the Gospel and the evolution of the community itself may have prompted various editions of the Gospel prior to its taking the form it now has in the New Testament. Commentators have long noted some features of the Gospel that suggest various layers of editing and transpositions in the sequence of John's story, although there is no strong consensus about how the text should be "restored" to its original order.[14]

Whatever speculation may be about the building blocks of the Fourth Gospel and its stages of formation, there is little doubt that the Passion story as it now stands is essential to the Gospel's portrayal of Jesus and his mission. The focus of our study is not on the question of John's sources. While some contact between John's account and that of the Synoptics cannot be ruled out, the comparisons we will draw between John and the other Gospels are intended to highlight the distinctive features of John's Gospel as it now stands in the New Testament rather than to demonstrate the possible sources of his material. And the issue of editorial stages, while not without significance in interpreting the Gospel, will, in fact, have a minor role to play in deciphering the meaning of the Passion account.

The method used in this study will be similar to that employed in the other three volumes of the series. We will approach John's Gospel not primarily to extract from it historical information about the actual circumstances of Jesus' Passion and death, nor to trace the formation of the Gospel in relation to early Christian history. John's account, in fact, does offer some intriguing information on these points such as the fact that Roman soldiers seem to play an active part in the arrest of Jesus (18:3), or that Jesus was first interrogated by the Father-in-law of the High Priest (18:13). But our focus is not here. Rather we will give attention to the structure and flow of John's narrative and to the literary features of each scene as he presents it to the reader, in order to

---

[14] To cite a few examples, there is an abrupt transition from Jerusalem to Galilee between chapter 5 and the beginning of chapter 6; the healing of the royal official's son in Capernaum (4:46-54) is counted as the "second" sign performed by Jesus whereas he had performed other signs in Jerusalem (2:23); in 14:31 Jesus seems to conclude his discourse at the last supper but then it continues to the end of chapter 17; and there seems to be two conclusions to the Gospel as a whole (20:30-31; 21:24-25).

draw from the text its theological message. There is little doubt that the Gospel presents the reader with a specific viewpoint about the manner and meaning of Jesus' death. That is what we will trace.

Part I will discuss John's overall structure and theological vision. We will then turn our attention specifically to the death of Jesus, tracing throughout the first seventeen chapters of the Gospel the characteristic themes, language, and turns in the story that John uses to prepare the reader for the Passion. The long farewell discourse of chapters 13-17 is unique to John and demands special attention because of its close connection to the Passion narrative.

Part II is a scene-by-scene study of John's Passion narrative, which covers the whole of chapters 18 and 19. A brief survey of chapters 20 and 21 illustrates how John carries over his presentation of the death of Jesus into his account of Jesus' resurrection appearances to the disciples at the conclusion of the Gospel.

Part III summarizes the major themes of John's Passion narrative, relates them to the overall theology of his Gospel, and suggests some of their theological and pastoral implications for today.

Writing the four volumes of this series has truly been a labor of love for me. That love was tested when some major and unexpected administrative duties crowded in on the timetable I had set for this project and I am relieved that my work is now complete. For first inviting me to write this series and for his wonderful encouragement and patience all the way through it, I am forever grateful to Michael Glazier. He has truly been a special gift to the world of Catholic publishing in this country and I am delighted that the Liturgical Press continues the tradition he has set.

Thanks, too, are due to Marylyn Welter, S.S.S.F. for her splendid work in preparing the manuscript and assisting on the indexes.

I want to dedicate this volume to Fr. Flavian Dougherty, C.P., Director of STAUROS International, a fellow Passionist and good friend, who died as this book was nearing completion. As the multitude of people who were touched by him and his great ministry can testify, in the strength of his life and the gracefulness of his death he exemplified the spirit of God's triumph which John's Gospel proclaims.

PART I

PREPARATION FOR THE PASSION

Within the Passion narrative itself, John deftly uses symbol, irony, and dramatic staging to proclaim the full meaning of Jesus' death. But long before that climactic part of the Gospel is reached, the reader learns that Jesus is to die at the hands of his enemies and that his death will be a triumphant proclamation of God's love for the world. From the opening stanzas of the Prologue (1:1-18), through the bitter controversies of Jesus' public ministry, and on into the final meal of Jesus with his disciples, John's Gospel keeps the impending death of Jesus in full view of the reader. This preparation in the Gospel, in effect, helps prepare the reader to probe beneath the surface of the Passion story and to detect there, like an ikon in words, its sense of triumph.

The goal of Part I of our study is, therefore, to trace these key passages and themes that lead the reader through the Gospel story to the Passion.

I. John's Theological Vision

Commentators on John have long noted that this Gospel manages to state its entire message in practically every passage of the Gospel. Like waves washing across a beach, John's understanding of Jesus is asserted and reasserted as the Gospel unfolds. While there is a "plot" to John's story and some movement of the drama from start to finish, the reader is confronted with the full picture right from the opening lines of the Gospel and it is restated in almost every subsequent scene. Before considering the framework of John's narrative and its key themes, it is helpful to attempt to state succinctly John's overall perspective or "theology."[1]

There is little doubt that the figure of Jesus stands at the epicenter of John's theology. The mission of Jesus and the world's response to it give the Gospel its meaning and energy. The vast canvas imagined in John's opening verses allows the evangelist to give cosmic and eternal dimensions to Jesus and his mission. He is the eternal Word springing forth from the very life of God before time began, arching into the created world and into the arena of time and space, there becoming "flesh" and revealing God's "glory" to the world.

To reveal God is the heart of Jesus' mission and, for John's Gospel, the key to understanding all that Jesus says and does.[2] Jesus takes "flesh"—that is, takes on a human nature and a human history—in order that God's consuming love for the world would be visible and comprehensible to the human world. Revealing God, in Johannine terms, is not the mere dissemination of information about God. What Jesus reveals is that God will not condemn the world but that God loves the world and intends to save it (3:16-17). Thus the message Jesus embodies is active, dynamic, compelling.

For John's Gospel, Jesus' humanity is not play-acting. The Word truly *becomes* "flesh" (1:14), becoming all that being human entails: a body, a history, relationships, encounter with suffering and death. The "flesh" of Jesus does not mask his divine origin and substance but enables it to be revealed to the world.

All of the dimensions of Jesus' life, therefore, become revelatory. His words, which John shapes into long, meditative discourses, become words of truth revealing God. His acts of healing become luminous "signs" manifesting God's "glory" and God's

---

[1] A helpful summary can be found in D. Harrington, *John's Thought and Theology* (Good News Studies 33; Wilmington: Michael Glazier, 1990); and the works of R. A. Culpepper, *Anatomy of the Fourth Gospel* (Philadelphia: Fortress, 1983), esp., 86–98; J. Jervell, *Jesus in the Gospel of John* (Minneapolis: Augsburg, 1984); R. Kysar, *John, The Maverick Gospel* (Atlanta: John Knox, 1976); R. Scroggs, *Christology in Paul and John* (Proclamation Commentaries; Philadelphia: Fortress, 1988), 55–102; D. Moody Smith, *John* (Proclamation Commentaries; Philadelphia: Fortress, 2nd rev. ed., 1986), 27–68.

[2] See J. T. Forestell, *The Word of the Cross* (Analecta Biblica 57; Rome: Biblical Institute Press, 1974); A. Lacomara, "The Death of Jesus as Revelation in John's Gospel," in *The Language of the Cross* (Chicago: Franciscan Herald Press, 1977), 103–28.

compassion. And, above all, Jesus' death—full assurance of his humanness—becomes the most eloquent sign of all, for in laying down his life for his friends Jesus reveals the incredible quality of God's love for the world (15:12-13).

While revelation of God's love is the driving force of Jesus' mission, it is, in one sense, not its ultimate step. The Word comes into the world and through death and resurrection returns to God. The return to God—not only of the Word but of all humanity—is the final purpose of Jesus' mission in the world. The communion of all being with God, with the same intensity and completeness that bonds God with Jesus, is the endpoint of the Johannine vision: "that they may all be one. As you, Father, are in me and I am in you, may they also be in us . . . that they may be one, as we are one." (17:21-22). To achieve that God-given destiny, the Risen Christ sends the power of the Spirit into the world.

But John's breathtaking vision does not succumb to easy triumphalism. The strength and tenacity of evil, the torpor sin inflicts even on the those with good will, lead to misunderstanding and rejection of the Word sent into the world. The manner in which John describes opposition to Jesus takes its cue from the Gospel's overall vision. His opponents prefer "darkness" to "light"; they make a pact with "lies" and "untruth"; they fail to comprehend where he is from or, worse, reject his testimony that he comes from God and assert that he is in league with Satan (8:48, 52). Ultimately they seek to kill him lest the magnetic force of his message draw the whole world after him (11:48).

The evangelist understands this opposition as the very nature of evil; the "world" loves its own and hates those whose spirit is not immersed in evil (14:18-19).[3] So the attacks of evil on Jesus are not unexpected but neither are they capable of thwarting the God-given mission of Jesus, the eternal Word of God. Paradoxically, the death which evil inflicts on Jesus in its effort to destroy

---

[3] John uses the term "cosmos" or "world" with a variety of meaning. At times, it has a neutral sense as when he refers to Jesus "coming into the world" or "leaving" the world—in these instances the "world" is simply the arena of human life (see, for example, 1:9; 16:21; 17:15). Or the world can be described as the object of God's redeeming love as in the important text of 3:16-17 and as created in the pattern of God's Word (1:10). But John also describes the "world" as the gathering point of values alien to the Gospel and therefore as rejecting Jesus and the disciples (1:10; 15:18-19; 17:14).

his mission becomes the very means by which his mission is achieved. The word of the cross—self-transcending love for the other to the point of death—is the very Word by which God chooses to reveal the divine love for the world. And, therefore, Jesus is not a victim on whom death is inflicted; no, he lays down his life "on his own accord" because "I have received this command from my Father" (10:18).

Emboldened by the Spirit (or "Paraclete" as John's Gospel prefers), the disciples are to be bound together by love and are sent to proclaim God's redeeming Word to the world as Jesus had done. They, too, would encounter opposition and hatred from the force of evil in the world, but, ultimately, they would overcome evil as Jesus had done and would be the instruments through which the unity of all being in God would be consummated.

It would be arrogant to claim that a few sentences capture all of the depth and power of John's message. But this description of John's vision does cover many of its features. In fact, it is not difficult to state the essential message of this Gospel because it is repeated over and over, in varying images and narratives, throughout the Gospel. John's message bears the unadorned simplicity of authentic contemplation. But the direct and uncomplicated nature of John's core intuition should not be mistaken for lack of depth.[4] The straining of modern scholarship to understand John's message is testimony enough to the subtlety of its words and symbols, and the depth of its message.

Nevertheless this core message of Jesus as revealing God's love for the world is sustained throughout the Gospel and stands behind John's interpretation of the Passion of Jesus.

II. John's Literary Style

The literary style of this Gospel goes hand in hand with its theological perspective. The substance of John's christology is his insistence that Jesus is the Word of God who is sent into the world to reveal God's redeeming love. That unique mission of Jesus ab-

---

[4] R. Kysar cites a proverb first applied to John's Gospel by Siegfried Schulz, ". . . it is a book in which a child can wade and an elephant can swim"; see, *The Fourth Evangelist and His Gospel* (Minneapolis: Augsburg, 1975), 6.

sorbs the attention of the Gospel and, as we have noted, is affirmed and reaffirmed on practically every page, giving the Gospel a certain repetitive flavor. Commentators have pointed out that almost all of Jesus' long discourses, characteristic of the Fourth Gospel, center on the Jesus' own claims to his unique identity. The miracle stories are interpreted by the evangelist as "signs" that also reveal the divine presence and authority of Jesus.

John's basic intuition that God's Word is revealed in and through the humanity of Jesus inclines the Gospel to exploit the use of symbolic language and the literary devices of misunderstanding, irony and paradox. Many of the Gospel's typical images and symbols serve this christology: thus Jesus is the "Way," the "Truth," "Life," "the Good Shepherd," "the Lamb of God," "Living Water" and "Bread of life" and so on. Jesus bears God's "name" and reveals it to the world (17:6).[5] Jesus' healings' do more than heal bodies and open eyes; these "signs" also proclaim his revelation to the world: so giving sight to the man born blind illustrates that Jesus is "the light of the world" (9:5) and raising Lazarus from the grave reveals that Jesus is "the Resurrection and the Life" (11:25).

Many of those who listen to Jesus misunderstand his words and become an opportunity for the Gospel to point to the deeper truth of Jesus and his message. Thus Nicodemus cannot understand how someone can be "born again" but Jesus knows the power of the Spirit (3:4). Nor can the "Jews" understand Jesus' words about the "bread from heaven," leading to a fuller statement of this theme on Jesus' part (6:25-59).

In the passion narrative, "irony" becomes a favorite Johannine device.[6] On the surface level and in the eyes of the characters in the drama Jesus appears to be a victim, but the reader knows this is not the case. Thus Pilate asks "What is truth?" while

---

[5] Several times in the Gospel, Jesus refers to himself with the formula "I am" (in Greek, *Ego Eimi),* evocative of the divine name in the Hebrew Scriptures and similar to revelation formulas in some ancient Greek religious texts. This designation can be used on its own (as in 18:5; see below, pp. 52-53), or in combination with a predicate: e.g., "I am the Bread of Life" (6:35). On this feature of John's christology, see R. Brown, *The Gospel According to John I-XII* (AB 29; Garden City: Doubleday, 1966), 533-38.

[6] See, especially, P. Duke, *Irony in the Fourth Gospel* (Atlanta: John Knox, 1985) and R. A. Culpepper, *Anatomy of the Fourth Gospel,* 165-80.

God's Truth stands before him (see below, 18:38). Jesus dies as a "king" enthroned on the cross, apparently defeated by his enemies, but his true identity is ironically proclaimed to the world in the placard Pilate fixes over the cross (see below, 19:19-22).

III. The Framework of John's Story

The repetitive character of John's Gospel does not mean that the unfolding of the "plot" or storyline of the Gospel is insignificant. The Fourth Gospel is, after all, a narrative, not a theological discourse.[7] And even though the overall message of John becomes apparent early in the text, there is a buildup of the story from its beginnings with the recruitment of Jesus' first disciples, through the mounting intensity of his public ministry and on to the climactic events of death and resurrection.

We will trace that storyline, giving particular attention to John's signals about Jesus' impending death.

A) PROLOGUE (1:1-18)

The Gospel begins with a poetic introduction that places Jesus' mission in an eternal and cosmic frame: the Word comes forth from God and is sent into the world, becoming flesh and, despite opposition, revealing God's glory and overcoming the power of darkness.[8] Even though these verses form a "prologue" to the Gospel proper they might be more accurately described as the intuitive "center" of the Gospel.[9] That is, the prologue states the core message of the Gospel as a whole and all of its other strands—the discourses, the miracles, the opposition to Jesus, his

---

[7] See R. A. Culpepper, *Anatomy of the Fourth Gospel,* 78-98, and R. Kysar, *John's Story of Jesus* (Philadelphia: Fortress, 1984).

[8] Whether or not the prologue was composed prior to, along with, or subsequent to the body of the Gospel is a matter of some debate. See the recent study of T. Tobin who situates the hymnic elements of the prologue in the context of Jewish wisdom theology, "The Prologue of John and Hellenistic Jewish Speculation," *Catholic Biblical Quarterly* 52 (1990) 252-69.

[9] See P. J. Cahill, "The Johannine *Logos* as Center," *Catholic Biblical Quarterly* 38 (1976), 54-72.

disciples, his death and resurrection—radiate from and find their explanation in this center.

From the contents of the prologue the reader knows Jesus' ultimate identity and knows that his mission will engender new life. But the reader also anticipates that darkness will attempt to overcome the Light (1:5) and that Jesus will be rejected by "his own" (1:11). Even in these opening strains of the Gospel, a note about the Passion of Jesus is sounded.

B) THE BOOK OF SIGNS (1:19–12:50)

The first half of John's Gospel which covers the public ministry of Jesus has often been entitled the "Book of Signs." Opposition to Jesus is muffled in the first four chapters but becomes a dominant theme from chapter five on.

The story begins in Bethany beyond the Jordan where John, the desert prophet, preaches and baptizes. Jesus approaches and is proclaimed by the prophet as "the Lamb of God who takes away the sin of the world" (1:29, 36). Faintly, yet distinctly, the evangelist once agains sounds a note about the death of Jesus— at the moment of Passover Jesus' life blood will be poured out for the sins of the world.[10]

Jesus draws his first disciples from those of John, and in Galilee these first followers begin to realize the mysterious origin of this "Son of Man" through whom the heavens are opened and God's angels ascend and descend (1:51).[11]

Jesus' public ministry begins to unfold in chapter two with the miracle of the wine at Cana, the first great "sign" that reveals Jesus' "glory" to the disciples (2:11). But the faith of the disciples is counterbalanced by the first explicit signs of opposition. At the first of three Passovers celebrated in this Gospel, Jesus goes to Jerusalem and there drives the merchants from the

---

[10] On John's use of Passover symbolism, see below, pp. 33–34.

[11] The Son of Man title in John expresses this mysterious origin of Jesus, the one who comes down from heaven to reveal God to the world; on this title in John, see B. Lindars, *Jesus Son of Man* (Grand Rapids: Eerdmans, 1983), 145–57; R. Scroggs, *Christology in Paul and John*, 69–72.

Temple.[12] The "Jews" challenge Jesus' authority and his reply alludes to his death: "Destroy this temple, and in three days I will raise it up." When the leaders misundertand his words—the first of many such instances in the Gospel—the narrator reveals the symbolic dimension of Jesus' words: "But he was speaking of the temple of his body. After he was raised from the dead, his disciples remembered that he had said this; and they believed the scripture and the word that Jesus had spoken." (2:22).

The gap between Jesus and the teachers of Israel is further illustrated in chapter three. Nicodemus, "a leader of the Jews," comes to Jesus "by night" to learn the meaning of his teaching but his questions reveal the depth of his ignorance (3:1-15). In typical fashion, the dialogue with Nicodemus becomes simply an opportunity for the evangelist to construct a discourse by Jesus.

Increasing opposition to Jesus is alluded to again at the beginning of chapter four. When Jesus hears that the Pharisees are agitated over the success of his ministry, he leaves Judea and goes to Samaria. His encounter with the Samaritan woman leads to her conversion of heart and to the acceptance of Jesus by the Samaritans of her city (4:1-42). From there he goes to Galilee and performs another sign, this time at Capernaum where he heals the son of an official (4:46-54).

But this apparent success of Jesus' mission seems only a respite, for the hostility against him which smoldered below the surface in the first four chapters bursts into flame in chapter five. Jesus decides to return to Jerusalem to celebrate a "feast" (5:1). The cure of the paralysed man at the pool of Bethzatha on a sabbath day has a curious impact. The man who was cured reports Jesus to the authorities and they take offense that Jesus had "violated" the Sabbath rest. For the first time in the Gospel we learn the intensity of their opposition and the reason for it: "For this reason the Jews were seeking all the more to kill him, because he was not only breaking the sabbath, but was also calling God his own Father, thereby making himself equal to God." (5:18).

---

[12] One of the major differences between John and the Synoptic Gospels is the geographical deployments of their stories. The Fourth Gospel has Jesus going back and forth to Jerusalem whereas in the Synoptics he makes one major journey to Jerusalem. In all four Gospels, Galilee is viewed more benevolently than Jerusalem. On the role of geography in the Gospels, see S. Freyne, *Galilee, Jesus, and the Gospels* (Philadelphia: Fortress, 1988).

The rest of the chapter is taken up with a long discourse of Jesus in which he reasserts his mission of revealing God to the world. The opponents reject Jesus' testimony, as they had that of John, because "I know that you do not have the love of God in you" (5:42) and they do not have God's word abiding in them (5:38).

A similar pattern is found in chapter 6. The miracle of the multiplication of the loaves (6:1-14) and the haunting manifestation of Jesus on the sea (6:16-21) is followed by the long discourse on the "bread of life" (6:25-59). The Jews "murmur" at Jesus because of his claim to be the "bread that came down from heaven" (6:41) and even many of his disciples take offense at his teaching and decide to leave him (6:60-66). For the first time we learn of Judas' treachery: " 'Did I not choose you, the twelve? Yet one of you is a devil.' He was speaking of Judas son of Simon Iscariot, for he, though one of the twelve, was going to betray him." (6:70-71).

The atmosphere of hostility continues to intensify in chapter 7. Jesus can no longer go about openly in Judea "because the Jews were looking for an opportunity to kill him" (7:1). Even his "brothers" begin to lose faith in him (7:5). Eventually Jesus decides to go up to Jerusalem for the feast of Tabernacles and John depicts the atmosphere as tense; the "Jews" are looking for him and the crowds are confused over what to make of him (7:10-13). In the Temple Jesus dialogues with the crowds, testifying that his teaching is from God and that his works are the work of God. Because they fear Jesus will sway the crowds, the Pharisees and chief priests send police to arrest him (7:32). But even the temple police are moved by Jesus' words and do not carry out their orders. When Nicodemus speaks on Jesus' behalf, the frustrated leaders brush him aside: "Surely you are not also from Galilee, are you? Search and you will see that no prophet is to arise from Galilee." (7:45-52).

After a night on the Mount of Olives (8:1) Jesus returns to the Temple and once again there is an angry confrontation with the authorities. The same issues that will erupt during the Passion narrative at the interrogation before the Sanhedrin are already stated with full force in this scene. The terms of the argument fit exactly into John's theological perspective. The dialogue opens with Jesus' declaration: "I am the light of the world" (8:12) but the Pharisees accuse Jesus of bearing witness only to himself and therefore his testimony is "not valid" (8:13). In the bitter exchange that follows Jesus constantly reasserts that he has come from God and that his words and actions are of God. But the leaders cannot understand his words and reject his deeds because they are mired in unbelief. They have the devil as their father and their deadly hostility to Jesus confirms this. "Whoever is from God hears the words of God. The reason you do not hear them is that you are not from God" (8:47).

This angry scene ends with the leaders taking up stones to kill Jesus but he "hid himself and went out of the temple" (8:59).

The white hot intensity of chapter 8 seems to bank only slightly in the next scene. Jesus' declaration that he is "the light of the world" (9:5) is illustrated in the miracle of restoring sight to the man born blind. But the theme of opposition to Jesus still holds the Gospel's attention. Because of his belief in Jesus, the Pharisees throw the man who was healed out of the synagogue. The scene ends with Jesus accusing the leaders of being blind and liable to judgment (9:39-41).

The exchange with the leaders continues in chapter 10 and once again the atmosphere crackles with open hostility between the leaders and Jesus. Jesus' discourse contrasts the "good shepherd" who lays down his life for the sheep (10:14-15) with the "hired hand" who abandons the sheep when there is danger. The theme of death runs through the chapter: Jesus "lays down" his life willingly and of his own accord in order to do the work the Father has given him to accomplish (10:11, 15, 17, 18). Because of Jesus' claim to be "one" with God the opponents take up stones and attempt to kill him once again but he escapes their threat (10:31, 39).

The climax of the Book of Signs comes in chapters 11 and 12. The raising of Lazarus is the final act of Jesus' public ministry. In liberating his friend Lazarus from death, Jesus enacts his identity as the "Resurrection and the Life" (11:25). But this great sign also triggers the final opposition to Jesus and puts in motion the plot that will lead to his death. Frustrated and fearful because of the magnetic power of Jesus' ministry, the leaders gather in council to decide what to do. Caiaphas the High Priest rises and gives his fateful statement: "You know nothing at all! You do not understand that it is better for you to have one man die for the people than to have the whole nation destroyed." (11:49-50). The ironic truth of this statement is so compelling that the narrator does not want the reader to miss it: "He did not say this on his own, but being high priest that year he prophesied that Jesus was about to die for the nation, and not for the nation only, but to gather into one the dispersed children of God" (11:51-52). The chapter ends with the council seeking a way "to put (Jesus) to death" and Jesus taking refuge in Ephraim with his disciples (11:53-54).

The stage is now ready for the Passion. Another Passover is at hand so six days before the feast Jesus returns to Bethany to the home of Lazarus to prepare for its celebration (11:55-12:1). At supper, Mary anoints the feet of Jesus with a pound of costly ointment and wipes them with her hair. Judas, whom John brands as a "thief," protests this lavish waste of the ointment but Jesus defends Mary and links the anointing to "the day of my burial" (12:3-8). The raising of Lazarus continues to have an impact. The chief priests decide to put him to death, too, because his return to life has caused such a stir in the crowds (12:9-11). And the Jerusalem crowds acclaim Jesus when he enters the Holy City because they had heard of his great miracle (12:12-19).

The Book of Signs ends as Greeks who had also come up for the feast seek out Jesus (12:20-22). Their presence seems to draw from Jesus a reflection on his impending death: The grain of wheat must fall into the ground and die in order for it to bear much fruit (12:24). Jesus' spirit trembles before the approach of the fateful hour but a voice from heaven thunders God's endorsement of Jesus and his mission (12:28). The voice, in turn, triggers Jesus' most eloquent statement on the meaning of his death: "Now is the judgement of this world; now the ruler of this world will be driven out. And I, when I am lifted up from the earth, will draw all people to myself" (12:31-32).

C) THE BOOK OF GLORY (13:1-20:31)

The evangelist signals a major turning point in the Gospel with the opening words of chapter 13: "Now before the festival of the Passover, Jesus knew that his hour had come to depart from this world and go to the Father. Having loved his own who were in the world, he loved them to the end." (13:1). The so-called "Book of Glory" covers events surrounding the Passion and resurrection of Jesus. In John this includes the long farewell discourse at the supper (chapters 13–17); the Passion narrative itself (chaps. 18–19); and the discovery of the empty tomb and the series of appearances to Mary and to the disciples (chapter 20).

In the Synoptic Gospels, such events as the anointing of Jesus, his predictions of betrayal, denial, and desertion on the part of the disciples, the last supper and the institution account, and the anguished prayer of Jesus in Gethsemane are all part of the Passion narrative itself and directly lead in sequence to the moment of the arrest.

But John's presentation is different. He seems to disperse his version of many of these preliminary events to other parts of his Gospel.[13] The Gethsemani prayers finds an echo in chapter 12 when Jesus says that "my soul is troubled" and a voice from heaven acclaims Jesus (12:27-30). The anointing takes place when Jesus goes to the home of Lazarus in Bethany six days before the passover (12:1-8).[14] There is no clear institution account in John but the words of Jesus in 6:51 seem to supply for it: ". . . the bread that I will give for the life of the world is my flesh." Prediction of Judas' betrayal comes early, at the conclusion of chapter 6 (see 6:64, 70-71).

In John's narrative the last supper dominates the five chapter segment of the Gospel immediately prior to the arrest of Jesus. Little attention is given to the meal itself; after the symbolic act of the footwashing, Jesus' long farewell discourse is the sole focus of the scene. It is a section of the Gospel without parallel in the Synoptics and contains some of the most characteristic language and themes of the Fourth Gospel.[15]

---

[13] R. Brown, "Incidents that are Units in the Synoptic Gospels but Dispersed in St. John," *Catholic Biblical Quarterly* 23 (1961) 143-60.

[14] In Mark 14:1 (see also Mt 26:6) the anointing takes place two days before passover and is included in the series of events that lead to the arrest; see D. Senior, *The Passion of Jesus in the Gospel of Mark* (Wilmington: Michael Glazier, 1984), 44-48.

[15] Luke, however, does depict Jesus giving something of a "farewell" discourse at the supper (Lk 22:14-38), much more than Mark or Matthew; see D. Senior, *The Passion of Jesus in the Gospel of Luke* (Wilmington: Michael Glazier, 1989), 49-83. On the key function of

Aware that Judas was about to betray him and realizing that his "hour" was at hand (13:1-3), Jesus girds himself with a towel and begins to wash the feet of his disciples. It is an example of loving service for them to imitate and a sign of the cleansing power of his death. Jesus knows the identity of his betrayer and when he give the apostate disciple a dipped morsel, it is as if a signal, permitting evil to do its work. "Satan entered into" Judas and he goes out in the night (13:27-30).

Jesus' long discourse now begins, occasionally punctuated by questions from the disciples. Characteristic themes of John's Gospel weave through these chapters. A dominant mood is one of leave-taking: Jesus is about to return to God and he instructs his disciples on what they are to do in his absence. Jesus will not abandon them but will send the Paraclete, the Spirit who will recall to the disciples Jesus' teaching, help them understand it, and embolden them to face opposition as they carry out their mission in the world.[16]

The disciples are to be obedient to Jesus' commands, to "abide" in him and his words (15:1-11), by imitating his own self-sacrificing love (14:21-24; 15:12-17). They are to love one another, as he has loved them. Jesus had loved them with the greatest love one can show a friend: to lay down one's life for the beloved (15:12-14). They are sent into the world as Jesus himself was sent (17:18) and they are to "testify" to Jesus (15:27). Therefore, they should expect from the "world" the same opposition and hatred that Jesus himself experienced (15:18-25; 16:1-4). But the Paraclete will be with them and sustain them (15:26; 16:13). Jesus will triumph over "the ruler of this world" (14:30; 16:33) and the Paraclete, too, will exercise judgment over the power of evil (16:8-11).

The "prayer" of Jesus in chapter 17 not only concludes the discourse but seems to give a sense of finality to Jesus' entire mission. Jesus "looked up to heaven" and said, "Father, the hour has come; glorify your Son so that the Son may glorify you . . ."

---

chapter 17 within the Johannine discourse and the Gospel itself, see E. Kasemann, *The Testament of Jesus* (Philadelphia: Fortress, 1968).

[16] On the Johannine theology of the Paraclete, see G. Burge, *The Anointed Community* (Grand Rapids: Eerdmans, 1987).

(17:1). Jesus has glorified God by "finishing the work that you gave me to do" (17:4); "I have made your name known to those you gave me from the world . . ." (17:6).

He prays for his disciples who will remain in the world, that God would protect them from the "evil one" (17:15) and "sanctify them in the truth" (17:17). He also prays for "those who will believe in me through their word" (17:20), that "they may all be one. As you, Father, are in me and I am in you, may they also be in us, so that the world may believe that you have sent me." (17:21).

Finally, Jesus asks that his disciples and all those who believe in God's Word through them will also return to God and "may be with me where I am, to see my glory, which you have given me because you loved me before the foundation of the world." (17:24). The last words of the prayer restate the entire mission of Jesus, a mission about to be accomplished in his death: "I made your name known to them, and I will make it known, so that the love with which you have loved me may be in them, and I in them." (17:26).

This exquisite prayer returns to the cosmic themes of the Prologue, framing John's narrative of Jesus' public ministry, and setting the stage for the climactic events of death and resurrection. The mission of the Word is about to be completed and he will return to the presence of the living God from whence he came (17:5; 1:1-2). The "Word" incarnate in Jesus (1:14) is now given to the disciples (17:14). And this same "Word" they will proclaim to the world (17:20).[17]

Now the events of the Passion can unfold. In chapters 18 and 19 John's Gospel has its closest parallels to the Synoptic Gospels. Judas leads a band of soldiers and temple police into a garden on the other side of the Kidron valley to arrest Jesus (18:1-11). He is taken first to Annas, the father-in-law of Caiaphas the High Priest, where he is interrogated and abused, and then to the High Priest himself (18:12-24). Peter meanwhile denies his discipleship when confronted by a maidservant and some of the bystanders

---

[17] While a dominant metaphor of the prologue, the image of Jesus as the "Word" of God does not emerge in the Gospel until chapter 17, yet it remains a leitmotif of Johannine christology throughout the Gospel, especially in the Gospel's portrayal of Jesus as the revealer of God; see, below, Part III, pp. 144–47.

(18:15-18; 25-27). Then the leaders bring Jesus to the praetorium to be tried by Pilate (18:28-19:16); the interplay between Pilate and the Jews, and the Roman's dialogue with Jesus, form a major part of John's Passion narrative. Finally, Pilate accedes to the wishes of the leaders and delivers Jesus to be crucified.

John's story lingers over details of the crucifixion scene: the placard Pilate fixes over the cross, despite the protests of the chief priests (19:19-22); the soldiers' decision not to rend his seamless tunic (19:23-25); Jesus' words to his mother and the beloved disciple (19:25-27); and Jesus' thirst (19:28-30). Jesus dies with words of triumph on his lips: "It is finished" (19:30).

Other strange occurrences command the attention of John's narrative as the Passion concludes: the soldiers do not break Jesus' legs to insure death but, instead, pierce his side, drawing out blood and water (19:31-37); and two hesitant disciples, Joseph of Arimathea and Nicodemus, give Jesus a hastened but still lavish burial (19:38-42).

The discovery of the empty tomb and resurrection appearance stories close out John's Gospel. Mary Magdalene is the first to find the tomb empty and she runs to tell Peter and the beloved disciple; they come to see for themselves (20:1-10). After they have returned home, Mary lingers near the tomb and the Risen Christ appears to her, proclaiming the news of his triumph: ". . . go to my brothers and say to them, I am ascending to my Father and your Father, to my God and your God" (20:11-18). That evening Jesus himself comes to the place where the disciples are holed up in fear; he reveals himself to them and breathes on them the gift of the Spirit, renewing their mission (20:19-23). Eight days later Jesus appears again, present this time is doubting Thomas, one of the Twelve who had refused to believe that Jesus was risen. Thomas is overwhelmed by Jesus' presence and acclaims the Risen Christ with the Gospel's most exalted confession: "My Lord and my God!" (20:26-29).

Once again the narrator breaks into the story and seems to sum up the purpose of the entire Gospel: ". . . these (things) are written so that you may come to believe that Jesus is the Messiah, the Son of God, and that through believing you may have life in his name" (20:30-31).

D) RETURN TO GALILEE . . . (21:1-25).

Despite the natural finale of 20:30-31, the story picks up again in chapter 21. The scene moves from Jerusalem to Galilee where the disciples have gathered. While Simon Peter and others are fishing, the Risen Christ appears mysteriously on the shore, guiding them to a marvelous catch and preparing a meal for them when they haul in the catch (21:2-14). In one of the Gospel's most touching scenes, Jesus draws a threefold declaration of love from the disciple who had denied him. Peter is also restored to his mission: he is to tend and feed Christ's sheep (21:19).

The haunting lake scene concludes ambiguously, drawing the reader's attention to the witness whose testimony is declared to be the basis of the story the evangelist narrates. Peter asks about the fate of the beloved disciple and is told by the Risen Jesus that it is not his concern if this disciple is to remain "until I come" (21:20-24).

Another summary statement ends the Gospel: "But there are also many other things that Jesus did; if every one of them were written down, I suppose that the world itself could not contain the books that would be written." (21:25).

LEADS TO THE PASSION

Our rapid survey of John's Gospel is enough to illustrate that the death of Jesus drives the story from start to finish. Of all the Gospels, John gives the most prominence to the strife between Jesus and his opponents. In the first chapter there are only distant echoes of eventual conflict, but as soon as Jesus begins his public ministry, that conflict breaks out into the open. By the time Jesus' ministry is in full stride his exchanges with the Jewish leaders are angry and ominous. When the Book of Glory begins (13:1), the reader is not surprised that death stands on the horizon.

But John's Gospel is not a series of mindless conflicts. In the Gospel's perspective, opposition is generated by the very nature of Jesus and his mission. Conflict breaks out where the meaning of the Gospel and the values of the world collide and the Passion is the final consequence of this collision.

To help prepare the way for a deeper understanding of the Passion, it may be useful to probe into some of the recurring themes that weave through the moments of opposition John records.

1. *The Death of Jesus as the Endpoint and Ultimate Expression of His Mission*

Fundamental to understanding the dynamics of John's Gospel is the realization that the death of Jesus is the ultimate expression of Jesus' mission from the Father; it is the final "sign" that reveals God's glory to the world.

That Jesus is "sent by God" is one of the Gospel's most insistent themes.[18] As we noted above, the purpose of that mission is to reveal God's redemptive love for the world.[19] For John the most eloquent statement of Jesus' revelation—his most effective sign—is his death out of love for others. There are a number of key texts in the Gospel that state this motif clearly. In the discourse with Nicodemus Jesus tells the Jewish teacher: "For God so loved the world that he gave his only Son, so that everyone who believes in him may not perish but may have eternal life. Indeed, God did not send the Son into the world to condemn the world, but in order that the world might be saved through him." (3:16-17).

In using the word "give" *(edōken),* John alludes to Jesus' death.[20] This is also made clear by the preceding text where Jesus states the first of three "lifting up" sayings, uniquely Johannine references to the death of Jesus: "And just as Moses lifted up the serpent in the wilderness, so must the Son of Man be lifted up, that whoever believes in him may have eternal life." (3:14-15). This is the very reason the Son of man has descended from heaven (3:13), that he would be lifted up on the cross and reveal God's love for the world.

---

[18] On this motif, see J. Comblin, *Sent From the Father* (Maryknoll: Orbis, 1979); T. Okure, *The Johannine Approach to Mission* (WUNT 31; Tübingen: Siebeck/Mohr, 1988), 24–28.

[19] See above, pp. 16–17.

[20] The term *paradidomi* and its derivitives, referring to God's deliverance of Jesus to death for the redemption of the world, becomes a quasi technical term in the Passion tradition; see, *"paradidomi"* in G. Kittel, *Theological Dictionary of the New Testament,* volume 2, pp. 169–73.

Other passages reinforce this fundamental Johannine theme which runs just below the surface on practically every page of the Gospel. In the Bread of Life discourse, for example, the Johannine version of the words of institution again proclaim that Jesus' death reveals God's redemptive love, this time using the image of heavenly bread and partaking of that bread: "I am the living bread that came down from heaven. Whoever eats of this bread will live forever; and the bread which I shall give for the life of the world is my flesh." (6:51). The image of the "Good Shepherd" also gives Jesus' death this salvific thrust: "The thief comes only to steal and kill and destroy. I came that they may have life, and have it abundantly. I am the good shepherd. The good shepherd lays down his life for the sheep." (10:10-11). The opening lines of the Book of Glory also state the theme unequivocally: "Now before the festival of the Passover, Jesus knew that his hour had come to depart from this world and go to the Father. Having loved his own who were in the world, he loved them to the end." (13:1).

The farewell discourse adds another key image to John's theology of the death of Jesus and helps guide the reader into the Passion story. Only in John's Gospel is Jesus' death interpreted as an act of friendship love: "This is my commandment, that you love one another as I have loved you. No one has greater love than this, to lay down one's life for one's friends." (15:12-13). The giving of one's life for another is the ultimate gift; no one can ask for more, or expect any more convincing sign of transcendent love.

Other passages express the same theme on a more symbolic level. The raising of Lazarus, for example, is an expression of Jesus' deep love for his friend from Bethany, a point the story repeatedly makes (see 11:3, 11, 35-36). But, at the same time, this miracle foreshadows Jesus' own death and is the trigger that springs Jesus' opponents into action and finally leads to his death (see 11:45-53). The raising of Lazarus, therefore, sums up Jesus' ministry in the Gospel and reveals the meaning of his own death: through the cross Jesus will rescue his beloved from death.[21] The

---

[21] On the raising of Lazarus as both summation of Jesus' ministry and a portent of his own death and resurrection, see B. McNeil, "The Raising of Lazarus," *Downside Review* 92 (1974) 269–275.

footwashing, which inaugurates the Book of Glory (see 13:3-20), also expresses the inner meaning of Jesus' mission by binding together in one symbolic act both the loving service and the ultimate cleansing Jesus' death will bring (see Jesus' words to Peter in 13:8: "Unless I wash you, you have no share with me.").

Passover

John also seems to use the motif of Passover in a similar fashion. The Baptist identifies Jesus as the "lamb of God who takes away the sin of the world" (1:29, 36), an apparent allusion to the lamb slaughtered for the passover ritual. The feast of Passover is noted several times in the Gospel: on the Passover Jesus makes his first public journey to Jerusalem to cleanse the temple, interpreted by the narrator as a sign that the Jerusalem temple would be replaced by Jesus' crucified and risen body which now becomes the new locus of communion with God (see 2:13-23). On the occasion of another Passover, Jesus multiplies the loaves and fish and gives his discourse on the Bread of life, the bread he would give "for the life of the world" (6:4, 51). The third Passover coincides with Jesus' death and John repeatedly signals its approach (see 11:55; 12:1; 13:1). All of this culminates in the moment of Jesus' death which takes place as the Passover lambs are being slaughtered in the Temple.[22] Jesus, the Lamb of God, brings to fulfillment the hopes of liberation expressed in the Passover ritual.[23]

As we have stressed throughout our discussion, the powerful meaning John attaches to the death of Jesus helps explain the Gospel's focus on the cross. The story moves forward to the Passion because it is there that the culmination of Jesus' mission will take place. And, at the same time, the centrality of Jesus' death, helps explain the weight John gives to the opposition to Jesus. In failing to recognize Jesus, the opponents turn away from ultimate truth. And in mounting their deadly plot against Jesus they unwittingly become instruments of God's grace because, para-

[22] See below, the discussion of John 19:14.

[23] See below, Part III, pp. 157–59.

doxically, in the very vengeance they wreak on Jesus the depth of God's love for the world will be demonstrated.

2. Death as Exaltation

Another undercurrent of John's Gospel carries the story forward to the Passion. In bringing his mission of revealing God's love for the world to the endpoint of the cross, Jesus also returns to God and is glorified. The cross of Jesus is both sign of death and sign of exaltation.[24]

John's conception of the Gospel drama has a certain "spatial" dimension to it. Jesus, the Son of Man who "comes down" from heaven, is "sent" from God. He "enters into the world" and "abides" there. Conversely, with death, Jesus "leaves" the world, "returns" to his Father, and "ascends" to where he was before.[25] As enfleshment is the Word's entry point into the world (see 1:14), so crucifixion becomes Jesus' paradoxical gateway to exaltation and glory at God's side.

"The Lifting Up of the Son of Man"

A number of key passages and themes expressing this perspective weave their way through the early part of the Gospel and prepare the reader to understand the full meaning of the cross in John. Primary among these are the "lifting up" sayings, one of the Gospel's most haunting images. Three times the Johannine Jesus refers to his death as a "lifting up," using the Greek verb *hupsothēnai.* The verb connotes both the crucifixion whereby Jesus' body is "lifted up" on the cross, and the exaltation of Jesus' ascent to glory at the right hand of God.

The first occurrence of this image is in the dialogue with Nicodemus: "And as Moses *lifted up* the serpent in the wilderness, so must the Son of man be *lifted up,* that whoever believes in him may have eternal life." (3:14). This text alludes to the strange in-

---

[24] G. Nicholson stresses the motif of ascent and glorification in John's theology; the "lifting up" of Jesus and the references to his "hour" are primarily to be understood as references to his exaltation by God; see G. Nicholson, *Death as Departure: The Johannine Descent-Ascent Schema* (SBL Dissertation Series 63; Chico, CA: Scholars Press, 1983).

[25] On this motif, see G. Nicholson, *Death as Departure,* and W. Meeks, "The Man from Heaven in Johannine Sectarianism," *Journal of Biblical Literature* 91 (1972), 44–72.

cident in Numbers 21 where the Israelites are punished for their disobedience by a plague of "fiery serpents." When they repent of their sins, God instructs Moses to fashion a bronze image of the serpent "and (to) set it on a pole; and everyone who is bitten shall look at it and live" (Num 21:8). Alluding to this incident, the Book of Wisdom stresses that the Israelites were cured not "by what they saw" but by God's power (Wis 16:7). John uses this evocative biblical image in a similar fashion.[26] The icon of Jesus' lifted up on the cross reveals God's love for the world (see 3:16-17, the key text that follows immediately on the "lifting up" saying).

A second instance is 8:28: "When you have *lifted up* the Son of Man, then you will realize that I am he, and that I do nothing on my own, but I speak these things as the Father instructed me." This saying is embedded in the bitter controversy of chapter 8.[27] The Jews accuse Jesus of bearing false testimony; in response Jesus reaffirms his fundamental mission: " 'I have much to say about you and much to condemn; but the one who sent me is true, and I declare to the world what I have heard from him.' They did not understand that he was speaking to them about the Father" (8:26-27). The "lifting up" on the cross is the message Jesus bears from the Father. If they could understand that "message"—something impossible for the unbelieving opponents—they would realize that Jesus bears the very name of God, "I am," and reveals God's redemptive love for the world.[28]

The third saying comes at the end of the Book of Signs, at a climactic moment immediately after Jesus prays in anguish about his impending death and a voice from heaven responds, reaffirming Jesus and his mission (see 12:27-28): "Now is the judgment of this world; now the ruler of this world will be driven out. And I, when I am *lifted up* from the earth, will draw all people to myself" (12:31-32).

The narrator makes clear that this is a reference to Jesus' death: "He said this to indicate the kind of death he was to die" (12:33). This final saying has a cosmic, triumphant scope to it: the Son

---

[26] See R. Burns, "Jesus and the Bronze Serpent," *The Bible Today* 28 (1990), 84–89.

[27] See above, pp. 23–24.

[28] On the "I am" sayings, see above, p. 19, n. 5.

of man is lifted up "from the earth" and will draw all people, a mood that will be picked up in the Passion narrative itself.[29] True to form, the "crowd" is unable to grasp what Jesus says: the law teaches that the Christ will remain forever so how, they ask, can the Son of man be lifted up? and who is this Son of man? (12:34). Jesus replies that only those who walk in the light can comprehend who he is and what work he has been given by the Father (see 12:35-50).

In many ways, the "lifting up" sayings parallel the Synoptic "Passion predictions," key sayings that punctuate the Gospel and through which Jesus foretells the suffering and eventual exaltation that the Son of Man must experience.[30] The Synoptic Passion predictions and the lifting up sayings in John give an orientation to the events of the Passion, providing for the reader in advance Jesus' own interpretation of the meaning of his death. A key point to note in John's Gospel is that the lifting up sayings portray the cross as both moment of death and moment of exaltation—a merger that is evident in the entire mood of the Johannine Passion narrative.

"Hour of Glory"

At several points in the Gospel Jesus refers to his death as his "hour." That sense of impending time gives the Gospel a mood of urgency and constantly carries the reader forward to the Passion.

The first instance is at the wedding feast of Cana; when the mother of Jesus requests that he do something about the wine running out, he replies: "Woman, what concern is that to you and to me? My hour has not yet come" (2:4). Although the reference is opaque at this point, the reader will soon learn the connection between this scene and the words of Jesus at the cross (19:26-27), the "hour" of his death.[31] Other texts make the tie to the hour of death quite explicit. In chapter 7 his enemies want

---

[29] See, for example, the implication of John 19:19-20; below, pp. 103–105.

[30] See, for example, Mark 8:31; 9:31; 10:33-34; see D. Senior, *The Passion of Jesus in the Gospel of Mark*, 28–30.

[31] See pp. 108–14.

to arrest him but were unable to lay hands on him "because his hour had not yet come" (7:30). A similar note is found in chapter 8 where Jesus' strong condemnation of the Pharisees in the Temple does not lead to his arrest because "his hour had not yet come" (8:20). And the Book of Glory begins with the solemn declaration: "Now before the festival of the Passover, Jesus knew that his hour had come to depart from this world and go to the Father . . ." (13:1).

Speaking of Jesus' death as a fateful "hour" echoes the sense of dramatic timing found in the Synoptic tradition where the death of Jesus is linked with the *kairos,* the fateful moment of the endtime when the world comes to an end and a new creation begins.[32] John, in fact, uses the notion of the "hour" to refer to the end of the world:

> "Very truly, I tell you, the *hour* is coming, and is now here, when the dead will hear the voice of the Son of God, and those who hear will live. For just as the Father has life in himself, so he has granted the Son also to have life in himself, and he has given him authority to execute judgment, because he is the Son of Man. Do not be astonished at this; for the *hour* is coming when all who are in their graves will hear his voice and will come out—those who have done good, to the resurrection of life, and those who have done evil, to the resurrection of condemnation." (5:25-29).

The phrase, "the hour is coming, *and is now here . . ."* collapses the expectation of the endtime into the present; what was anticipated for the end of the world is taking place *now* in the person and mission of Jesus, a typical Johannine perspective.[33] This same anticipation of the endtime may influence other instances where John uses the notion of "hour" (see, for example, 4:21, 23; 16:2, 4), including the references to Jesus' death. As Jesus dies, so, too, does the old world and a new one is born.

---

[32] This is especially true of Matthew's Gospel; see the discussion of Mt 26:18 in D. Senior, *The Passion of Jesus in the Gospel of Matthew,* 60-61.

[33] On John's so-called "realized" eschatology, see R. Brown, *The Gospel According to John I-XII,* pp. CXV-CXXI.

This perspective is reinforced by the link between the "hour" of the death of Jesus and the notion of "glory."

This becomes apparent towards the end of the Book of Signs. The request of some Greeks who want to see him appears to trigger in Jesus an awareness of his approaching death: "The *hour* has come for the Son of Man to be *glorified*" (12:23). At that same moment Jesus' spirit is filled with troubled prayer: "Now my soul is troubled. And what shall I say? "Father save me from this *hour?* No, for this reason I have come to this *hour.* Father, *glorify* your name. Then a voice came from heaven, "I have *glorified* it, and I will glorify it again." (12:27-28). "Hour" and "glory" are linked again at the beginning of Jesus' great prayer in chapter 17, immediately before the beginning of the Passion narrative: "After Jesus had spoken these words, he looked up to heaven and said, "Father, the *hour* has come; *glorify* your Son so that the Son may *glorify* you . . ." (17:1).

The notion of "glory" and "to glorify" have rich theological meaning in John and are closely connected with his basic interpretation of Jesus as the revealer of God. Jesus' entire life and work "glorify" God, that is, give God due honor and praise (see, for example, "I glorified you on earth by finishing the work that you gave me to do" 17:4). And, in turn, God "glorifies" Jesus by giving him victory over death: ". . . so now, Father, glorify me in your own presence with the glory that I had in your presence before the world was created" (17:5).

"Glory" is the manifestation of that divine presence which is worthy of praise and honor. God obviously is the bearer of "glory" (5:44; 11:4, 40; 12:43) but in John's Gospel Jesus himself is suffused with God's "glory" and reveals it to the world. This image expresses a basic intuition of John's christology and first appears in the Prologue: The Word who is made flesh takes up his dwelling in the community, "full of grace and truth," and "we have seen his glory, the glory as of a father's only son" (1:14). This is what the disciples of Jesus manage to see in his great sign of abundant wine at Cana (2:11) and what will be manifest to Mary and Martha when Jesus raises their brother from the dead (11:40, 45). And the full dimensions of Jesus' astounding glory will be revealed to the disciples when they see him standing in triumphant union with God (17:24).

In binding the "hour" of the death of Jesus with the notion of "glory," especially in the latter part of his Gospel, John prepares the reader for the paradox of the cross. It is a moment that seems to rush forward with terrible power, but it will also be a moment of exaltation and triumph when the glory of God will stream through the crucified Jesus.

3. *Response to Jesus: Faith and Opposition*

As the Gospel story unfolds and Jesus reveals himself in word and sign, people respond in very different ways—some in faith, some with deadly opposition, while others seems suspended between belief and fear. This part of the story line, too, helps prepare the reader for the events of the Passion.

Believing in Jesus

Those who believe are those able to recognize that Jesus is sent from God and bears God's message of love for the world. The followers of John the Baptist are intrigued by the Galilean who comes to the Jordan and, after abiding with him a while, come to believe in him (1:35-41). When Jesus changes the water into wine, a sign of God's abundance, the disciples see through this sign to the "glory" of God manifest in Jesus. The Samaritan woman and the citizens of her town (4:1-42), the official at Capernaum whose son Jesus cured (4:46-54), the man born blind whose eyes are opened (9:38), the witnesses to the raising of Lazarus (11:45)—all of these characters in the Gospel "believe" in Jesus. They are not afraid "to come to the light" (3:21).

The Hostility of Unbelief

But in sharp contrast, many others refuse to believe in Jesus and, as we had noted above, their hostility to Jesus escalates as the Gospel story unfolds.[34] John's Gospel, in fact, depicts opposition to Jesus much more vividly than the other Gospels do. The Prologue announces this motif—"he came to what was his own, and his own people did not accept him" (1:11)—and particularly

---

[34] See above, pp. 22-25.

from chapter five on Jesus' opponents are intent on destroying him. The "Jews" seek to kill him after he heals the man at the pool of Bethzatha, because he "not only was breaking the sabbath, but was also calling God his own Father, thereby making himself equal with God" (5:18). In chapter 7 we learn that Jesus could not travel openly in Judea "because the Jews were looking for an opportunity to kill him" (7:1). At the feast of tabernacles when Jesus goes to Jerusalem, the "chief priests and Pharisees sent temple police to arrest him" (7:32); that determination is asserted again near the end of the chapter when some of the Jerusalem crowd "wanted to arrest him, but no one laid hands on him," much to the frustration of the leaders (7:43-45). In chapter 8, where the hostility between Jesus and his opponents becomes white hot, Jesus tells them: ". . . but now you are trying to kill me, a man who has told you the truth that I heard from God" (8:40). In chapter 10, the "Jews" take up stones in order to kill Jesus (10:31) and when they later try to arrest him, he escapes to the transjordan (10:39-40).

The raising of Lazarus is the final straw: the chief priests and Pharisees summon the council and they formally decide that Jesus must die "for the people" (11:47-53). "From that day on," the narrator observes, "they planned to put him to death." The way to the Passion is now clear.

The Demonic

Right from the start of John's Gospel, the enemies of Jesus are intensely hostile and want to destroy him. The opponents are one-dimensional, practically becoming symbols of unbelief and even of evil itself. Standing behind the unyielding hostility of the leaders is, in John's perspective, the face of the demonic. John's Gospel, curiously, has no exorcisms, a point of major contrast with the Synoptic Gospels.[35] But Jesus' combat with evil which the Synoptic Gospels express by means of the exorcism stories finds its echo in the Fourth Gospel in the bitter conflicts between Jesus and his opponents. Jesus' enemies accuse him of being in

---

[35] Exorcisms play a major role in the ministry of Jesus in all three Synoptics, but particularly in the Gospel of Mark.

league with Satan (7:20; 8:48; 10:20), but Jesus himself has the decisive word: "You are from your father the devil, and you choose to do your father's desires. He was a murderer from the beginning and does not stand in the truth, because there is no truth in him." (8:44).

The driving force of Satan behind the opposition to Jesus will find its culmination in Judas, one of the disciples. The betrayer of Jesus seems to personify the demon: " 'Did I not choose you, the twelve? Yet one of you is a devil.' He was speaking of Judas son of Simon Iscariot, for he, though one of the twelve, was going to betray him." (6:70-71). At the beginning of the Book of Glory, the demon makes its move: "The devil had already put it into the heart of Judas son of Simon Iscariot to betray him . . ." (13:2). When Jesus, who knew what was taking place, shares with the betrayer a morsel at the meal, it becomes a signal that the demonic treachery could begin: "After he received the piece of bread, Satan entered into him. Jesus said to him, 'Do quickly what you are going to do.' " (13:27). As Judas leaves, he steps into the darkness—a vivid Johannine touch (13:30).

What Jesus will therefore confront in the Passion is the power of evil itself. It wears many masks: Jesus' opponents, Judas, and ultimately the power of Rome which condemns Jesus to death. There is no real middle ground. This epic struggle between God and evil, between life and death, between faith and unbelief, between light and darkness is the cosmic level on which much of Johannine theology runs.

John's tendency to make the opposition to Jesus symbolic of evil itself has important consequences for interpreting this Gospel. The tendency to abstraction also works to merge the opponents of Jesus into a single category: "the Jews." John does give a prominent role to the "Pharisees" and the "chief priests," often in combination. But distinctive of John is the labeling of Jesus' opponents as "Jews," a labeling, as we will note below, that has had some terrible consequences in subsequent Christian interpretation of the Gospel.[36] Where Mark, Matthew, and Luke will speak of "Pharisees and Scribes" or other specific opposition

---

[36] See below, Part III, pp. 155-57.

groups, John frequently uses "the Jews."[37] John is not consistent in this; "Jews" can be used in a neutral or even a positive sense. But, similar to John's use of the term "world," the usual sense is negative because the "Jews," like the world itself, refuse to believe in Jesus and stand in opposition to his mission.[38]

Searching for the Truth

There are a few characters in the Gospel that seem to stand suspended between those who believe and those who are hostile. Nicodemus is a prime example.[39] He comes to Jesus "by night," a "man of the Pharisees," a "leader of the Jews" (3:1-2). He is anxious to learn from Jesus whom he respects as a "teacher who has come from God" (3:2) but he lacks "understanding" and apparently is not ready to receive the full meaning of Jesus' testimony (3:10-11).

Nicodemus is one of the few minor characters to make repeated appearances in the Gospel. The frustrated attempt of the chief priests and Pharisees to have Jesus arrested during the feast of Tabernacles is another occasion when this would-be disciple makes a cameo appearance. When the leaders berate the police for failing to arrest Jesus, Nicodemus dares to speak on Jesus' behalf: "Our law does not judge people without first giving them a hearing to find out what they are doing, does it?" (7:51). The Gospel's description of Nicodemus at this point catches the ambiguity perfectly: "Nicodemus, who had gone to (Jesus) before, and who was one of them . . ." (7:50); so, too, does the caustic response of the leaders to Nicodemus' intervention: "Surely you are are not also from Galilee, are you? Search and you will see that no prophet is to arise from Galilee." (7:52).

The last appearance of Nicodemus will be at the burial of Jesus, where the Gospel seems to imply that the triumph of the cross

---

[37] See, for example, John 5:10, 15, 16; and the "Jews" as the opponents in chs. 6, 8. In chapter 9, the Gospel refers alternately to "Pharisees" (9:13, 15, etc.) and "the Jews" (9:18, 22). On this point see, R. Fuller, "The "Jews in the Fourth Gospel," Dialog 16 (1977) 31-37.

[38] On the term "world" in John, see above, p. 17, n. 3.

[39] See J. Bassler, "Nicodemus in the Fourth Gospel," *Journal of Biblical Literature* 108 (1989) 635–46, and the discussion below, pp. 130–33, 163.

will finally dissolve the hesitation of this man who cautiously searches for the truth (see 19:39).

Even the disciples are not without their struggles to believe. Although they "see" Jesus' glory at Cana, their faith can waver and even break. Some of them find Jesus' words about the "Bread from heaven" too difficult to bear and they leave him (6:60-66). Judas will fall victim to Satan and betray Jesus. And even though Peter affirms his faith in the strongest possible terms (6:68-69), and claims that he would die for Jesus, he will first deny his discipleship (13:37-38).

The Passion of the Community and the Judgment of the World

The Gospel warns that the Passion—the moment when the full force of evil will be unleashed on Jesus—will also take its toll on the community. The disciples, too, will undergo the withering assault of evil and have to endure the cold hatred of the world—not only as they stand by Jesus during his Passion but as they carry out his mission in the world. If his words about the bread of life cause offense, much more offense can be taken by his death on the cross (6:62). In his final discourse, Jesus warns that the world will "hate" the disciples just as it hated him (15:18; 17:14) and just as the world persecuted Jesus it will persecute them (15:20). The disciples would be "driven out of the synagogues" and "indeed, an hour is coming when those who kill you will think that by doing so they are offering worship to God" (16:2). They, like their Teacher, would have to "lose" their life to save it, and "hate" their life in this world in order to gain it forever. Following Jesus meant learning the lesson of the grain of wheat that had to fall to the earth and die, so that it could bear much fruit. (12:4-26).

While the reader of the Gospel braces for the onslaught of evil as the Passion is about to begin, there is also the promise of triumph. Jesus will exercise judgment over the "world," and when the fateful hour comes, he exults in his victory: "Now is the judgment of this world, now shall the ruler of this world be cast out" (12:31).

These leads to the Passion drive the reader forward to the climactic hour of the Gospel. While John's Gospel has a cyclic rhythm and seems to repeat its characteristic themes over and over, the force of narrative remains. As the reader turns the pages of John's Gospel, the message is clear: only with Jesus' death will the story of the Word made flesh reach its terrible and triumphant conclusion.

PART II

THE PASSION OF JESUS

Introduction

Jesus has completed his ministry of "signs" and words. The bitter controversies with his opponents have taken their course. Jesus has bid farewell to his disciples and steeled them for the hour that is at hand. Now the Passion can begin.

John begins the Passion with the arrest of Jesus (18:1-11). At this point, the Fourth Gospel seems to converge with the Synoptic accounts. But as we will chart in this next major section of our study, each scene of the Passion bears a strong Johannine signature.

There are four major scenes in John's Passion story: (1) The first (18:1-11) is in the "garden" across the Kidron valley where the arrest will take place. (2) The scene then shifts to an interrogation, first before Annas, the father-in-law of the High Priest, and then to the High Priest himself, Caiaphas (18:12-27). While Jesus takes on his interrogators, Peter will deny that he is a disciple. (3) The third and most extensive scene of the Passion is the trial before Pilate (18:28-19:16). John stages the action of this section with great skill, alternating the reader's focus from private conversations between Pilate and his prisoner inside the praetorium to confrontations with the Jewish leaders and people outside. (4) The final episodes take place on Golgotha (19:17-42), first the dramatic events at the cross and then the burial of Jesus in a garden near where he was crucified.

Each scene of the Passion is drenched with John's literary skill and theological perspective. Our goal is to examine each episode and draw from it the evangelist's message.

I. The Arrest: Jesus Confronts His Enemies (18:1-11)

John's Passion narrative begins with a powerfully staged scene that quickly displays to the reader the evangelist's dramatic skill and theological perspective. The arrest of Jesus triggers a sharp confrontation between Jesus and his enemies, between God's Word to the world and the forces of disbelief and evil. This same drama has run like a deep current throughout John's Gospel and will now erupt in the climactic moment of Jesus' death.[1]

[1] After Jesus had spoken these words, he went out with his disciples across the Kidron valley to a place where there was a garden, which he and his disciples entered. [2] Now Judas, who betrayed him, also knew the place, because Jesus often met there with his disciples. [3] So Judas brought a detachment of soldiers together with police from the chief priests and the Pharisees, and they came there with lanterns and torches and weapons. [4] Then Jesus, knowing all that was to happen to him, came forward and asked them, "Whom are you looking for?" [5] They answered, "Jesus of Nazareth." Jesus replied, "I am he." Judas, who betrayed him, was standing with them. [6] When Jesus said to them, "I am he," they stepped back and fell to the ground. [7] Again he asked them, "Whom are you looking for?" And they said, "Jesus of Nazareth." [8] Jesus answered, "I told you that I am he. So if you if you are looking for me, let these men go." [9] This was to fulfill the word that he had spoken, "I did not lose a single one of those whom you gave me." [10] Then Simon Peter, who had a sword, drew it, struck the high priest's slave, and cut off his right ear. The slave's name was Malchus. [11] Jesus said to Peter, "Put your sword back into its sheath. Am I not to drink the cup that the Father has given me?"

Unlike the Synoptic Gospels which begin their Passion narratives with Jesus' anointing in Bethany and Judas' treacherous negotiations with the religious leaders, John's account plunges directly into the action of Jesus' violent nighttime arrest. This

---

[1] See above, Part I, pp. 39–44.

opening scene immediately introduces the reader to the tone of paradox that runs throughout John's Passion story. On one level of the story we have the ominous rituals of violence and apparent defeat: betrayal by a friend; the threatening presence of armed soldiers; a nighttime arrest of an innocent man; summary interrogation, trial and torture; finally, a public execution and a hasty burial. The genius of John's Passion narrative is that these gruesome realities of seeming defeat and death do not dominate the story. Woven in and through the account of Jesus' suffering and death is another, more dominant mood: Jesus, God's powerful Word, is triumphant over death. He is not a victim from whom life is violently taken, but one who gives his life freely as an act of love for the world.

We can trace this blend of death and triumph in almost every element of this opening scene.

The basic setting of the arrest scene is very similar to the Synoptic accounts. The lingering farewell scene of Jesus with his disciples that began in the supper room in chapter 13 with the symbolic act of washing of their feet, and continued with a long, meditative discourse in chapters 14–17 is now concluded. Jesus and his disciples leave the supper room and walk from the elevated western part of Jerusalem (the probable location of the meal) down the steep incline that meets the southern edge of Temple wall, and move across the sharp cleavage of the Kedron valley to an enclosed garden on the slopes of the Mount of Olives (18:1).[2] John situates the opening scene of the Passion story on this sacred hillside with its breathtaking view of the Temple and David's City—the very place where Jewish tradition expected the end of the world to come.

Jesus and his disciples apparently intended to stay the night here. Jewish law required that Passover pilgrims spend the night in Jerusalem. To accomodate the large number of visitors to the city, it was understood that the boundaries of the city included the Mount of Olives. Although John does not say exactly why Jesus and his disciples go to the garden, this may be the implicit rationale. In any case it was a place well known to Jesus and his

---

[2] John accurately describes the wadi that separates the temple mount from the Mount of Olives to the East as the "winter-flowing" *(cheimarros)* Kedron.

disciples (18:2). In the Synoptic Gospels, Jesus goes to a secluded place ("Gethsemane") to pray for strength before his ordeal. In a sense, John has taken care of this preparatory prayer in chapter 12 and in the discourse of chapters 14–17.[3] Jesus' readiness to face his death is tested with the sudden arrival of Judas and an armed band of soldiers who come to apprehend him. The scene will focus on this dramatic confrontation between Jesus and his enemies.

John escalates the drama of arrest by the forces he has arrayed against Jesus. At the head of the list is Judas. John has the betrayer take the initiative in his act of treachery. Judas knows where Jesus will be that night and goes and procures a band of soldiers and police and leads them to Jesus (18:3). John's Gospel has no sympathy whatsoever for Judas and sees behind his terrible apostasy the face of the demon.[4] From his first appearance in the Gospel Judas is identified as the betrayer whose deeds are inspired by evil. At the end of the Bread of Life discourse, Jesus tells his disciples: " 'Did I not choose you, the twelve? Yet one of you is a devil?' He was speaking of Judas son of Simon Iscariot, for he, though one of the twelve, was going to betray him." (6:71). In John's version of the anointing at Bethany, it is Judas (not the disciples in general, as in Mark and Matthew) who protests the waste of the precious ointment and his motives are venal: "He said this not because he cared about the poor, but because he was a thief; he kept the common purse and used to steal what was put into it" (12:5-6).

John underscores the perversion of Judas and his dominance by demonic power at the beginning of the Book of Glory. During the final supper of Jesus and his disciples, ". . . the devil had already put it into the heart of Judas son of Simon Iscariot to betray him" (13:2). Jesus himself is fully conscious of Judas' apostasy. After washing the feet of his disciples, he seems to grieve over Judas' sin:

---

[3] On John's creative reinterpretation of Jesus' final prayer before his Passion, see D. Stanley, *Jesus in Gethsemane* (New York: Paulist, 1980), 223–68.

[4] See above, Part I, pp. 40–42.

"I am not speaking of all of you; I know whom I have chosen. But it is to fulfill the scripture, 'The one who ate my bread has lifted his heel against me.' I tell you this now, before it occurs, so that when it does occur, you may believe that I am he . . . After saying this Jesus was troubled in spirit, and declared "Very truly, I tell you, one of you will betray me." (13:18-19, 21).

When asked by the Beloved Disciple—"Lord, who is it?" (13:25)—Jesus identifies Judas as the betrayer: " 'It is the one to whom I give this piece of bread when I have dipped it in the dish.' So when he had dipped the piece of bread, he gave it to Judas son of Simon Iscariot. After he received the piece of bread, Satan entered into him. Jesus said to him, 'Do quickly what you are going to do.' " (13:26-27). Judas' sin of avarice and betrayal is compounded by his violation of tablefellowship with Jesus, an underlying motif of chapters 13–15.

In the arrest scene, the evangelist evokes the mood of Jesus' last conversation with Judas by using the symbolism of darkness. In accepting the morsel from Jesus at the supper, Judas' terrible sin is unveiled; he leaves the table and goes out into the "night" (13:30).[5] There is little question that John alludes to the "night" in order to symbolize the demonic power of disbelief and death which drives Judas' sinfulness and which stands in radical opposition to the one who is God's Light (9:5). Judas and the forces who come to arrest Jesus also come in the darkness, bringing "lanterns and torches and weapons" (18:3). The mood is reminiscent of the words of Jesus in Luke's arrest story: "But this is your hour, and the power of darkness" (Luke 22:53).[6]

The atmosphere of threat is also heightened by the list of forces whom Judas leads into the garden. John mentions a "detachment of soldiers together with police from the chief priests and the

---

[5] Curiously, John depicts the disciples themselves as being unaware of why Judas suddenly leaves the meal: "Now no one at the table knew why he said this to him. Some thought that, because Judas had the common purse, Jesus was telling him, 'Buy what we need for the feastival'; or, that he should give something to the poor." (13:28-19).

[6] Luke gives a significant role to the power of the demonic in the Passion story and throughout his Gospel and Acts, see D. Senior, *The Passion of Jesus in the Gospel of Luke* (Wilmington: Michael Glazier, 1989), 31–35, 92–93, 171–73; also, S. Garrett, *The Demise of the Devil: Magic and the Demonic in Luke's Writings* (Minneapolis: Fortress, 1989).

Pharisees" (18:3). The word used for the "detachment of soldiers" is *speira*. This Greek word was consistently used to translate the Latin term for a "cohort," one tenth of a Roman Legion or about 600 men. It could also designate a "manipulus," a smaller segment of a cohort numbering about 200 soldiers. This terminology, and the reference to an "officer" or "tribune" in 18:12, another technical word used for a Roman officer in charge of a cohort, leave little doubt that John intended to include Roman soldiers in the band that comes to arrest Jesus.

None of the other evangelists refer to Romans at this point in the Passion story. There is much debate whether or not it is historically plausible that Roman soldiers would be involved in the arrest of a Jewish suspect and then lead him for interrogation to the deposed High Priest Annas (see 18:13).[7] Whatever the historical complications, it is clear that John does include Romans among the array of forces against Jesus. This not only prepares for the later confrontation between Jesus and Pilate that will dominate John's Passion story (see 18:28–19:16) but escalates the dramatic scale of the arrest scene. Jesus is confronted by the whole array of his enemies: Gentile and Jewish.[8]

John describes the Jewish authorities as "police from the chief priests and the Pharisees." Historically this may refer to the temple police retained by the Sanhedrin to maintain order in the Temple precincts. John is the only evangelist to note the presence of "Pharisees" in the Passion story.

This combination of "chief priests and Pharisees" is characteristic of John's Gospel, each time used at a moment when the

---

[7] See the discussion in R. Brown, *The Gospel According to John XII-XXI* (AB 29; Garden City: Doubleday, 1970) 807–808, 814–817. The actual historical role the Romans might have played in the arrest of Jesus is difficult to determine. It is not improbable that there may have been, for pragmatic purposes, some collaboration even at this early stage between Roman and Jewish authorities in the volatile atmosphere of pre-revolutionary Jerusalem. On the situation at this period, see the interesting reconstruction of R. Horsley, *Sociology and the Jesus Movement* (New York: Crossroad, 1990).

[8] "Just as at Jesus' trial he [the evangelist] gathers together on one stage the Jewish leaders and the Roman judges, and just as he burdens the Jews more heavily (cf. 19:11b), so he gives a share to the representatives, of the gentiles, of the faithless world opposed to God . . . : in the same way, even at the time of the arrest, he would have Jesus confront the whole unbelieving cosmos." R. Schnackenburg, *The Gospel According to St. John.* Vol.3 (New York: Crossroad, 1982), 223.

religious authorities decide to take action against Jesus. During the feast of Tabernacles many of the crowds had marveled at Jesus' words and powerful signs: "When the Messiah comes, will he do more signs than this man has done?" (7:31). But this provoked the anger of authorities and so the "chief priests and Pharisees" sent "officers" to arrest Jesus (7:32). But instead of seizing Jesus the officers themselves are dazzled by his teaching, further igniting the anger of the authorities (7:45-45-52). Jesus' great sign of raising Lazarus from the dead again stokes the leaders' anger and reinforces their unrelenting determination to destroy Jesus: "What are we to do? This man is performing many signs. If we let him go on like this, every one will believe in him, and the Romans will come and destroy both our holy place and our nation . . . So from that day on they planned to put him to death." (11:47-53).[9]

Judas' solidarity with the enemies of Jesus at the moment of the arrest is tersely reaffirmed in 18:5—"Judas, who betrayed him, was *standing with them.*" This deadly array stands over against Jesus in the nighttime of the garden: a fallen disciple, the violent power of Rome, and the anger of the religious authorities.

All of this serves as a foil to the majestic power of Jesus. Jesus is not caught off guard. Consistent with his portrayal throughout the Gospel, John emphasizes Jesus' full knowledge of what was about to take place. Jesus is not to be seized as a helpless victim; he "comes forward" and boldly confronts the powers of darkness: "Whom are you looking for?" (18:4). John's Gospel loves such probing questions. Jesus asks a similar question of two disciples of the Baptist who are intrigued by Jesus at the beginning of the Gospel (1:38) and of Mary Magdalene as she stands weeping at the tomb (20:15).

The enemies of Jesus answer: "Jesus of Nazareth" (18:5) Jesus' own response and its impact clearly reveal the symbolic dimension John gives this entire scene. "I am he," Jesus declares and, at his words, the armed band "stepped back and fell to the ground" (18:6). At the very moment one might expect an unarmed victim to crumple, John portrays Jesus as in full command of

---

[9] On this passage, see above, pp. 24-25.

the situation. The entire mood of this scene harkens back to a statement of Jesus fundamental for all of John's Passion account: "For this reason the Father loves me, because I lay down my life in order to take it up again. No one takes it from me, but I lay it down of my own accord. I have power to lay it down, and I have power to take it up again. I have received this command from my Father" (10:17-18).

Jesus' words to Judas and the police are literally: *egō eimi,* "I am." The impact of these words on the enemies of Jesus confirms this as another instance in the Gospel where Jesus bears the mysterious and revealing name ascribed to God in the Hebrew Scriptures, "I am."[10] Once again Johannine paradox is in play. John had already linked the moment of betrayal with the revelation of Jesus' divine name at the supper when he had predicted Judas' apostasy: "I tell you this now, before it occurs, so that when it does occur, you may believe that *I am" (egō eimi;* 13:19). Now in the terrible darkness of discipleship betrayal and as Jesus' freedom is about to be violated by his enemies, the luminous divine nature of Jesus shines through and overwhelms those who would destroy him.

The captors of Jesus recoil from this divine authority and fall to the ground (18:6), a typical biblical reaction to a manifestation of the divine presence.[11]

The impotence of the forces of darkness is clear; it is Jesus who must take the initiative. He repeats the question, "Who are you looking for?" and identifies himself as the Jesus of Nazareth they seek (18:7). The contrast with the Synoptic accounts is vivid: in their versions, Judas comes forward to offer Jesus a treacherous kiss to identify him to his captors.[12] Not so in John. And the Jo-

---

[10] See above, p. 19, n. 5.

[11] Some commentators speculate that John alludes here to such Old Testament texts as Isaiah 11:4, which speaks of the Messiah as smiting "the earth with the rod of his mouth, and with the breath of his lips he shall kill the wicked." (R. Schnackenburg, *The Gospel According to St. John,* Vol. 3, 225) or Psalm 56:9, "Then my enemies will retreat on the day when I call. This I know, that God is for me." (C. K. Barrett, *The Gospel According to St. John* [Philadelphia: Westminster, 2nd ed., 1978] 520).

[12] Note, however, that Matthew has Jesus first speak to Judas (Mt 26:50) before the arrest takes place, and Luke has Judas "draw near to Jesus to kiss him" but Jesus' own words intervene before the betrayer can carry out the sign (Lk 22:47).

hannine Jesus also protects his disciples so that they have no need to flee.[13] With superb control, Jesus offers himself in place of his disciples: ". . . if you are looking for me, let these men go" and wins their freedom (18:8).

The evangelist sees this protective action as the fulfilment of Jesus' own word: "I did not lose a single one of those whom you gave me" (18:9). There is no promise of Jesus in the Gospel identical to these words but it is strongly reminiscent of such earlier sayings as 6:39, ". . . and this is the will of him who sent me, that I should lose nothing of all that he has given me," or 17:12, "While I was with them, I protected them in your name, that you have given me. I guarded them, and not one of them was lost except the one destined to be lost, so that the scripture might be fulfilled."

The care of Jesus for his disciples and his fierce determination to lose none of them is evocative of the Shepherd imagery of chapter 10.[14] The Johannine Jesus interprets his death as the shepherd's willingness to "lay down his life for the sheep" (10:11, 15). The commitment of Jesus the Shepherd to the life of his flock enables him to declare: "My sheep hear my voice. I know them, and they follow me. I give them eternal life, and they will never perish. No one will snatch them out of my hand. What my Father has given me is greater than all else, and no one can snatch it out of the Father's hand" (10:28-29).

It is indicative of John's strong christology that Jesus' own words are spoken of in terms of "fulfillment"—a term reserved in other parts of the New Testament for the Hebrew Scriptures.[15] But in John's Gospel, the sayings of Jesus already bear the aura of authority the early community attributed to the Old Testament.

---

[13] In Mark 14:50-52 all of the disciples flee, one of them naked. In Mt 26:56 the disciples also flee, a point which the evangelist connects with fulfillment of the Scriptures. No mention of their flight is found in Luke; perhaps because Jesus has prayed for their perseverance at the supper (see Lk 22:31-32). On this, see D. Senior, *The Passion of Jesus in the Gospel of Luke*, 71-75.

[14] See J. Forestell, *The Word of the Cross* (Analecta Biblica 57; Rome: Biblical Institute Press, 1974), 83; B. Lindars, *The Gospel of John* (New Century Bible; Greenwood, SC: Attic Press, 1977), 542.

[15] See B. Lindars, *New Testament Apologetic: The Doctrinal Significance of the Old Testament Quotations* (London: S.C.M. Press, 1973).

Peter

A final vignette about discipleship completes the arrest scene. The disciples have taken a passive role in the drama to this point. But as the arrest is about to take place "Simon Peter" draws his sword and cuts off the right ear of "Malchus," the slave of the high priest (18:10). This violent incident is found in all of the Gospels (Mk 14:47; Mt 26:51; Lk 22:50) and each evangelist interprets the scene with slightly different nuances.[16] But only John's Gospel identifies Peter as the one who uses the sword and gives a name to his victim. John shares with Luke the bit of information that the sword severs the *right* ear.[17]

Peter's violent intervention is strongly rejected by Jesus: "Put your sword back into its sheath. Am I not to drink the cup that the Father has given me?" (18:11). Although the four Gospels differ in the details of this scene they share one fundamental perspective, one sometimes neglected in discussions of this text. In each case Jesus refuses to endorse the use of violence on his own behalf. In John's scene, Jesus reminds Peter that he must "drink the cup which the Father has given" him. The "cup" stands here as a symbol of Jesus' death. That is clearly the case in the Synoptics where Jesus prays that "this cup" (of his death) might pass from him (Mk 14:36; Mt 26:39; Lk 22:42). While John has not referred to the "cup" in this manner earlier in his Gospel, the force he gives to the words of Jesus at the moment of his death— "I thirst"—evoke this same symbolism.[18] Jesus is determined to drink the "cup" of his death because this act of ultimate friendship love—and not the use of violent force—is capable of revealing God's own redemptive love for the world.

---

[16]See the discussion in D. Senior, *The Passion of Jesus in the Gospel of Luke,* 89–93.

[17] There is some speculation whether this detail is significant. Did John (and Luke) have access to more detailed historical traditions about this? Or are such details a result of the tendency of later tradition to add to the narrative? Is the mutilation even more hideous because it is the *right* ear? And is it significant that the mutilation is of the high priest's slave, thereby preventing him from attending the priest in the inner confines of the temple because of this disability? None of these questions can be answered with any confidence; see the discussion in M. McVann, "Conjectures About a Guilty Bystander: The Sword Slashing in Mark 14:47," *Listening* [River Forest, IL] 21 (1986) 124–137.

[18] See below, commentary on 19:28, pp. 115–18.

In other words, John draws a sharp contrast between the exercise of power used by the enemies of Jesus who come with weapons (18:3), and the liberating power of Jesus' own life and death. This fundamental contrast between two opposing worlds of values—revealed so vividly in the arrest scene—will be stressed again when Jesus confronts Pilate at the trial: "My kingdom is not from this world. If my kingdom were from this world, my followers would be fighting to keep me from being handed over to the Jews. But as it is, my kingdom is not from here." (18:36).[19]

The scene concludes with Jesus' enemies taking him captive. Once again the evangelist lists the array of forces determined to destroy Jesus: "the soldiers, their officer, and the Jewish police" (18:12). Representatives of the whole world—Gentile and Jew, secular power and religious leader—stand against God's Word. And hovering behind in the darkness is the demonic power that had seized hold of Judas and led him to betray Jesus. But the reader knows well, even in the darkness of the garden, that these forces of death which now seize Jesus will not overwhelm him.[20]

---

[19] See below, pp. 80–83.

[20] On John's use of irony here, see R. A. Culpepper, *Anatomy of the Fourth Gospel* (Philadelphia: Fortress, 1983), 174–75.

II. Jesus and Peter Tested: The Interrogation of Jesus by Annas and Caiaphas, and the Denials of Peter (18:12-27)

The Johannine Passion story picks up momentum as Jesus is bound as a prisoner and taken to be interrogated by Annas and Caiaphas. While having some parallels with the Synoptic accounts, this scene remains unique to John's Gospel.

[12] So the soldiers, their officer, and the Jewish police arrested Jesus and bound him. [13] First they took him to Annas, who was the father-in-law of Caiaphas, the high priest that year. [14] Caiaphas was the one who had advised the Jews that it was better to have one person die for the people.
[15] Simon Peter and another disciple followed Jesus. Since that disciple was known to the high priest, he went with Jesus into the courtyard of the high priest, [16] but Peter was standing outside at the gate. So the other disciple, who was known to the high priest, went out, spoke to the woman who guarded the gate, and brought Peter in. [17] The woman said to Peter, "You are not also one of this man's disciples, are you?" He said, "I am not." [18] Now the slaves and the police had made a charcoal fire because it was cold, and they were standing around it and warming themselves. Peter also was standing with them and warming himself.
[19] Then the high priest then questioned Jesus about his disciples and about his teaching. [20] Jesus answered, "I have spoken openly to the world; I have always taught in synagogues and in the temple, where all the Jews come together. I have said nothing in secret. [21] Why do you ask me? Ask those who heard what I said to them; they know what I said." [22] When he had said this, one of the police standing nearby struck Jesus on the face, saying, "Is that how you answer the high priest?" [23] Jesus answered, "If I have spoken wrongly, testify to the wrong. But if I have spoken rightly, why do you strike me?" [24] Then Annas sent him bound to Caiaphas the high priest.
[25] Now Simon Peter was standing and warming himself. They asked him, "You are not also one of his disciples, are you?" He denied it and said, "I am not." [26] One of the slaves

of the high priest, a relative of the man whose ear Peter had cut off, asked, "Did I not see you in the garden with him?" [27] Again Peter denied it, and at that moment the cock crowed.

John's Passion narrative continues to be dominated by a sharp, uncompromising conflict between Jesus and the forces of unbelief. Jesus is confronted by the summit of Jewish religious leadership: Annas the deposed but still powerful former Highpriest and his son-in-law Caiaphas, currently reigning as High Priest. As in the previous scene, the figure of Peter seems to hover between the stark choices of life and death which the Passion story presses on the reader. The apostle follows Jesus into the court of the high priest but begins to lose his nerve when identified by the servants as one of Jesus' disciples. Throughout the scene, Jesus remains the dominant, triumphant figure even as the forces of death coil to strike at him.

HISTORICAL AND LITERARY ISSUES

There are a number of complex historical and literary questions connected with this scene. We can discuss some of them briefly before focusing on the content of John's presentation.

First of all, the nature of the proceedings against Jesus is not clear. John's account omits any semblance of a formal trial: there are no accusations, no witnesses, and and no formal verdict—all of which are found in the Synoptics.[1] John mentions two separate interrogations, one by Annas and one by Caiaphas, but narrates only the first. Mark and Matthew both report a late night session of the Sanhedrin (Mk 14:53-15:1; Mt 26:57-27:1). But in John, more evidently than in the Synoptics, these sessions are preliminary hearings to gather evidence against Jesus rather than formal legal proceedings. Only the high priest takes a role in the

---

[1] Compare, Mk 14:53-65 and the parallels in Matthew and Luke. Even in the case of the Synoptics, however, it is probable that what is described is an interrogation or hearing, not a formal "trial." On this issue, see D. Senior, *The Passion of Jesus in the Gospel of Mark,* 88-90; W. Grundmann, "The Decision of the Supreme Court to put Jesus to Death (John 11:47-57) in its context: Tradition and Redaction in the Gospel of John," in E. Bammel & C.F.D. Moule (eds.), *Jesus and the Politics of His Day* (Cambridge: Cambridge University Press, 1985), 295-318.

interrogation. John may conceive of the full Sanhedrin being present as Jesus is questioned, since in 18:28 the "they" who lead Jesus to Pilate seems to refer to the full body of the Jewish leaders.

John is the only evangelist to mention an interrogation by Annas.[2] Josephus the Jewish historian informs us that Annas was high priest from A.D. 6 to 15, when he was deposed by the Romans. We also know that Annas and his family remained a powerful force: five of his sons eventually reigned as high priests. John's account seems to reflect this historical reality since the arresting party (including the Roman soldiers) brings Jesus first to Annas rather than to Caiaphas who was the current high priest. Perhaps because Annas had been deposed by the Romans, the Jews continued to respect Annas as the authentic high priest. But in John 11:49 Caiaphas seems to take a decisive role in the deliberations of the Sanhedrin and John notes that he is indeed the currently reigning high priest as the interrogation scene begins (18:13).

John's account does not offer any explanation for Annas' role other than stating that he was "the father-in-law of Caiaphas, the high priest that year" (18:13). Even more confusing is the reference in 18:19 where "the high priest" begins to interrogate Jesus. Is this Annas or Caiaphas? If John means the latter, then the conclusion of the scene in verse 24, where Jesus is sent bound to "Caiaphas the high priest," is incomprehensible.

Some interpreters—ancient and modern—have tried to solve some of the problems of this scene by suggesting that the text of John has been jumbled through the fusing and editing of previous sources. For example, an ancient Syriac translation and some Fathers of the church had already attempted to restore what they supposed was the original version by moving verse 24 to the beginning of the scene, thereby having Jesus immediately transferred from Annas to Caiaphas.[3] This allows the mention of the "high

---

[2] Luke mentions Annas two times, each in conjunction with Caiaphas: at the beginning of the Gospel when he situates Jesus' public ministry "in the high-priesthood of Annas and Caiaphas" (3:2) and in Acts where the Sanhedrin, including "Annas the high priest and Caiaphas . . ." gather to interrogate Peter and the Jerusalem apostles (Acts 4:5-6). Note that in Acts, Luke describes "Caiaphas and John and Alexander" as members of "the high-priestly family."

[3] See a discussion of this material in R. Brown, *The Gospel According to John XIII-XXI*, 820-21.

priest" in verses 15, 16, 19, and 22 to refer to Caiaphas, not Annas. While convenient, this solution cannot explain why John's text would have given a role to Annas at all or why an early scribe would have created such confusion in the first place by transposing the reference to Caiaphas.

Several reasons, in fact, may have converged to forge the text in its present form. Here, as in other parts of the Gospel, the evangelist may be in touch with traditions that have historical probability and are independent of those found in the Synoptic Gospels. It is likely, for example, that Annas may have continued to play an influential role in the religious affairs of Judaism at this period. He may also have been popularly addressed as the "high priest" even though he did not formally hold that office. Annas' initial interrogation of the prisoner could have been useful to gain a preliminary reading of Jesus' guilt or to help decide what strategy to use in presenting him to the Sanhedrin and ultimately to the Roman Governor.

At the same time, it is unlikely that Jesus would have undergone a formal trial led by either Annas or Caiaphas. The "trials" before the Sanhedrin reported in the Synoptics were probably formal hearings, helping the religious leaders determine if and on what basis Jesus should be delivered for trial before the Roman authorities. Thus John's reporting of interrogations by Annas and Caiaphas, without formal charges or witnesses, has the ring of historical accuracy.

Some of the rough edges or apparent gaps in John's account may also reflect the literary and theological tendencies of the Gospel. John had anticipated the "verdict" of the Sanhedrin earlier in the Gospel. Before the Passion had even begun, the Sanhedrin under Caiaphas' leadership had taken formal action against Jesus. Agitated by the popular reaction to Jesus' climactic sign of raising Lazarus from the dead, the chief priests and the Pharisees "gathered the council" to decide what response to make to this wonder worker: "What are we to do? This man is performing many signs. If we let him go on like this, every one will believe in him, and the Romans will come and destroy both our holy place and our nation" (11:47-48). At that moment Caiaphas delivered to the Sanhedrin his ironic prediction of Jesus' redemptive death: "You know nothing at all! You do not understand that it is better for you to have one man die for the people than to have the whole nation destroyed." (11:49-50). From that day, John notes, "they planned to put him to death" (11:53).

The evangelist clearly wants the reader to remember this intervention of Caiaphas as the interrogation scene of the passion begins. In 18:14 he recalls that "Caiaphas was the one who had advised the Jews that it was better to have one person die for the people."

As we will point out below, the whole atmosphere of the interrogations is also reminiscent of chapters 8 and 10 of the Gospel where Jesus had vehement clashes with the leaders. By the time the Passion story arrives, the reader already knows the verdict the opponents will bring against Jesus.[4] Thus the Passion story needs only to evoke those earlier "trials." John will reserve the formal trial narrative for the encounter with Pilate, the dominant scene of the Passion where all of the hostile forces of the Gospel story gather against Jesus (see below, 18:28-19:16).

Interrogation by the High Priest

John reports that the "high priest" (presumably Annas) questions Jesus about "his disciples and about his teaching" (18:19). Throughout John's Gospel, Jesus' personal identity as the unique revealer of God is the stumbling block for the leaders.[5] In the Roman trial, they will charge Jesus with being "a criminal" (18:30) and protest his claim to be a "king" (19:12) and "the Son of God" (19:7).

But in this scene Annas' interrogation is concerned with Jesus' *teaching* and its impact on his followers. Some interpreters suggest that the high priest accuses Jesus of being a false prophet but others believe the interrogation mirrors the experience of the Johannine church where followers of Jesus were being persecuted for their allegiance to Jesus and for their proclamation of the Gospel.[6]

---

[4] See R. Brown, *The Gospel According to John XIII-XXI*, 833-34. John anticipates in earlier parts of his Gospel a number of Passion events: e.g., the words of institution (6:51); the Gethsemane prayer (12:27-30; 17:1-5); the anointing (12:1-8).

[5] See, for example, 7:46-49 and the series of sharp exchanges in 8:19-39.

[6] For example, R. Kysar, *John* (Augsburg Commentary; Minneapolis: Augsburg, 1986), 273; R. Schnackenburg, *The Gospel According to St. John,* Vol. 3, 238.

But the high priest's question also swings the scene into the issue of "truth" and here a familiar Johannine theme emerges.[7] In the Synoptic accounts Jesus remains almost completely silent before his accusers but, similar to the arrest scene, the Johannine Jesus openly challenges his opponents.

Jesus' response, with its emphasis on speaking openly and bearing witness to the truth before the world, links the interrogation scene with chapter 8. There, too, the atmosphere was charged with confrontation between Jesus and the Jewish leaders, and there, too, were references to the Jesus' arrest and his Passion (see 8:20, 28, 59). Jesus proclaimed himself to be "the light of the world," the Revealer whose very being discloses the ultimate truth of God's presence in the world (8:12). This taps into one of the most fundamental currents of John's Gospel: Jesus is the incarnate "Word," who has come from God to reveal God's redemptive love for the world.[8] But the opponents of Jesus—again taking their symbolic Johannine role as the forces of unbelief and ultimate falsehood—fiercely reject Jesus' claim to be the "truth": "You are testifying on your own behalf, your testimony is not valid" (8:13).

Despite the attacks of his enemies, John notes, Jesus continued to teach in the temple "but no one arrested him, because his hour had not yet come" (8:20). That "teaching" continues throughout the Gospel, amplified not only by Jesus' signs and words but by his very being. Jesus sums up this open ministry of truth in his response to Annas:

> "I have spoken openly to the world; I have always taught in synagogues and in the temple, where all the Jews come together; I have said nothing in secret." (18:20)

John does report Jesus' teaching in the synagogue (6:59) and repeatedly in the temple (e.g., 2:13-22; 7:14; 8:2; 10:22-30).[9] But

---

[7] On the theme of "truth" in John's Gospel, see I. de la de la Potterie, *La vérité dans saint Jean* (Analecta Biblica 73; Rome: Biblical Institute Press, 1977) and his comments on this passage in *The Hour of Jesus* (Staten Island: Alba House, 1989), 47–50.

[8] See above, Part I, pp. 31–33.

[9] Note the similarity of this saying to Mark 14:48-49 and parallels: "Have you come out

this summation of Jesus' teaching activity has a broader sweep—
catching up the heart of Jesus' entire mission as the revealer of
God. It is for this reason the disciples call Jesus "teacher and
Lord" (13:13).

In the sharp clash reported in chapter 8, the symbolic role played
by the opponents in John's account is clearly evident. Their opposition to Jesus is demonic in origin, representing unbelief and
ultimate rejection of the truth:

> "Why do you not understand what I say? It is because you can-
> not accept my word. You are from your father the devil, and
> you choose to do your father's desires. He was a murderer from
> the beginning and does not stand in the truth, because there
> is no truth in him. When he lies, he speaks according to his
> own nature, for he is a liar and the father of lies. But because
> I tell the truth, you do not believe me. Which of you convicts
> me of sin? If I tell the truth, why do you not believe me? Who-
> ever is from God hears the words of God. The reason you do
> not hear them is that you are not from God." (8:43-46)[10]

This fierce exchange influences the denial scene. Annas' dis-
believing questions to Jesus are symptoms of unbelief and the
highpriest's failure to recognize the truth. "Why do you ask me?"
Jesus demands, "Ask those who heard what I said to them; they
know what I said" (18:21). The blow struck by one of the officers
is another sign of the opponents' failure to recognize "Truth."[11]
Jesus is slapped because his answer is taken as disrespect for the
high priest (see Exodus 22:28) but Jesus' words reassert his witness to the truth: "If I have spoken wrongly, testify to the wrong.
But if I have spoken rightly, why do you strike me?" (18:23).[12]

---

with swords and clubs to arrest me as though I were a bandit? Day after day I was with
you in the temple teaching, and you did not arrest me."

[10] The same accusation is found in John 10:25-27: "I have told you, and you do not believe.
The works that I do in my Father's name testify to me; but you do not believe, because you
do not belong to my sheep"; see also 7:16-18, 24.

[11] Unlike the Synoptics, John does not have an account of Jesus' mockery by the guards
at the conclusion of the Jewish "trial" but this hostile act of the officer during the interrogation is reminiscent of that abuse.

[12] Note the similarity to Jesus' self-defense in 7:23-24: ". . . are you angry with me because

The conclusion to the scene, with Annas sending Jesus bound as a prisoner to Caiaphas (18:24), demonstrates that the high priest is, indeed, incapable of hearing the Truth and falls under the condemnation of Jesus's words.

Peter's Denial

Another story shadows the unyielding confrontation between Jesus and the high priest. By framing the interrogation of Jesus with the account of Peter's denials, John continues an effective technique used by Mark and Matthew.[13] While Jesus boldly proclaims his identity and mission before the high priest, Peter crumples in fear and denies his discipleship. But, equally important, the scene also subtly contrasts the unyielding hostility of those who reject Jesus with the hapless wavering of the apostle who struggles with weakness and fear but not to point of definitive apostasy.

Each of the Gospels contains the remarkable story of Peter's denials. While the other disciples are swept off the scene, Peter lingers, at a safe distance, and follows Jesus up to the point of his interrogation by the high priest. This puts the dramatic spotlight on Peter's failure which takes place as if in slow motion and in full view of the reader.

John adds a new twist to the story. Along with Peter there is "another disciple" who also follows Jesus to the place of the interrogation (18:15). This disciples is "known to the high priest" and for this reason was able to gain entry for Peter and himself into "the court of the high priest" (18:15-16). We learn nothing more about the identity or the fate of this "other disciple"; he plays no further role in the scene. Commentators on John have debated whether or not this "other disciple" should be identified with the "beloved disciple" who has such an intriguing and important role in the Fourth Gospel.[14] This "beloved disciple"

I healed a man's whole body on the sabbath? Do not judge by appearances, but judge with right judgment."

[13] See D. Senior, *The Passion of Jesus in the Gospel of Mark,* 86–88; also, C. Evans, " 'Peter Warming Himself': The Problem of an Editorial Seam," *Journal of Biblical Literature* 101 (1982) 245–49.

[14] See discussion in R. Brown, *The Gospel According to John XIII-XXI,* 822–23, who con-

was last mentioned in conjunction with Peter, a frequent pairing in the Gospel.[15] At the supper, the "disciple whom Jesus loved" was reclining next to Jesus and passed along Peter's question about the identity of the betrayer (13:22-26). The same beloved disciple will reappear at the crucifixion scene where Jesus' entrusts his mother to him (see 19:26-27).

Although the identification remains a bit vague, it is probably this same disciple who plays a minor role in the denial scene. The Gospel does not speculate any further on the relation of the Beloved Disciple to the high priest so we have no way of knowing the origin of this tradition or its historical probabilities. For John's narrative, in any case, this relationship provides a rationale for Peter being able to enter into the courtyard of the high priest. Only through the intercession of the other disciple is Peter allowed to enter the gate, thus setting the stage for the denials (18:15-16).

The woman (literally, the "gatekeeper"), seeing Peter in the company of the "other disciple," makes what seems an unthreatening observation: "You are not also one of this man's disciples, are you?" (18:17) The question is repeated in 18:25.   The maid's slightly incredulous question may imply that a companion of a trusted friend of the high priest would not be an associate of the troublemaker just arrested and brought in for questioning. The question puts Peter on the spot. It is not a direct accusation (the woman expects him to say *"no"),* but to answer truthfully would expose Peter to the same fate as Jesus. And the question is put to him in the courtyard of the high priest and at the very moment Jesus is a prisoner under interrogation! Thus denial is relatively easy while asserting his identity as a a disciple could have disastrous consequences.

Peter chooses denial: "I am not" (18:17). With superb irony John formulates his statement in a manner that recalls Jesus'

siders the evidence inconclusive; R. Schnackenburg, *The Gospel According to St. John,* vol. 3, who is emphatic that this is not the Beloved Disciple, 234–35 and F. Neirynck who argues persuasively that it *is,* in *Evangelica* (F. Van Segbroeck, ed.; BETL 50; Leuven: Leuven University Press, 1982), 335–64. On the "beloved disciple" and his possible relationship to Johannine tradition, see M. Hengel, *The Johannine Tradition* (Philadelphia: Trinity Press International, 1989).

[15] In addition to the supper text and the possible reference in the denial scene, see 20:2-10; 21:7, 20–23.

challenging self-identification to the arresting band in the garden (18:5): *egō eimi* ("I am").[16] While Jesus publicly proclaims his identity (and his mission), even in the face of death, Peter, out of fear, will choose to deny his identity and his discipleship.

At this point John breaks off the Peter story to turn back to Jesus standing before the High Priest. The "slaves and police" gather around a charcoal fire in the court to warm themselves (see Mark 14:54 and Luke 22:55) and Peter joins them. The stage is set for the second and third denials but the narrator now concentrates on Jesus' interrogation by Annas (18:19-24). The vivid contrast between master and disciple jumps off the page. Jesus speaks "openly to the world" and not in secret (18:20). Fear drives Peter to conceal his true identity.

John returns to the Peter story in verse 25 ("Now Simon Peter was standing and warming himself . . ."). Twice more the disciple will deny his identity. The servants and guards gathered at the fire repeat the question of the doorkeeper: "You are not also one of his disciples, are you?" (18:25). Peter repeats his denial. The third confrontation escalates the drama because now there is a positive identification of Peter, and the wording of the accusation reflects this. A relative of Malchus, the high priest's servant whom Peter had attacked in the garden, hones in on Peter: "Did I not see you in the garden with him (Jesus)?." In Mark and Luke the sign that gives Peter away is the fact that he is a "Galilean" (see Mark 14:70; Luke 22:59); Matthew may imply the same reason when the bystander identifies Peter on the basis of his "accent" (Mt 26:73). But John draws on his own story line to tighten the noose around Peter: his act of violence in the garden comes back to haunt him (see 18:10-11).

For a third and final time Peter denies his discipleship. At that very moment, John notes, "the cock crowed" (18:27). That haunting signal in the night brings the reader back to Jesus' prophetic words at the last supper. There Peter had insisted on his unswerving loyalty to Jesus, even as Jesus had warned that there would

---

[16] On this formula in John, see above, p. 19, n. 5. Some commentators question whether John intends this link between Peter and Jesus' statement, but coming on the heels of the arrest and given the contexts of public testimony in the face of threat, it seems most probable that John intends this ironic connection.

come a time when the disciples would not be able to follow him: "Where I am going, you cannot follow me now; but you shall follow afterward."[17] But Peter's bravado was not dented: "Lord, why can I not follow you now? I will lay down my life for you." Jesus answered, "Will you lay down your life for me? Very truly, I tell you, before the cock crows, you will have denied me three times" (13:36-38).

There is no resolution of Peter's fate at this point in the Passion story. But Jesus' words at the supper—"but you will follow afterward"—are taken up in the resurrection appearance stories of chapters 20 and 21.[18] Peter's low intensity faith will be evident again at the tomb. The beloved disciple is moved to faith when he sees the empty tomb and the neatly folded burial cloth (20:8) but Peter remains baffled. Peter's redemption comes only in chapter 21 when his threefold denial of Jesus will be healed by a threefold declaration of love drawn from the hapless disciple by the Risen Christ. At this point, Peter will once again be confirmed in his mission of following after Jesus (21:15-23).

The entire interrogation scene serves well John's christology and his teaching on discipleship. The triumphant Christ that strides through the Johannine Gospel is apparent even in the darkest moments of the Passion. Jesus is bound as a prisoner and about to be condemned to death, but he speaks boldly to his interrogators and fearlessly proclaims his mission of truth to the world. John, unlike the Synoptic Gospels, does not portray Jesus as the Isaian Suffering Servant, absorbing in silence the violence of his persecutors. Jesus is, rather, the light of the world boldly challenging the power of darkness. The negative role played by Jesus' opponents serves as a foil to John's christology. Their hostile rejection of the truth is interpreted by John as symptoms of a demonic spirit, incapable of recognizing truth and therefore condemned to falsehood.

The example of Peter's cowardice in the face of threat also highlights Jesus' triumphant and courageous declaration of his mis-

[17] Note the similar prediction of discipleship failure in 16:32, "The hour is coming, indeed it has come, when you will be scattered, every one to his home, and will leave me alone. Yet I am not alone because the Father is with me."

[18] See below, pp. 136, 141-44.

sion. But the injection of Peter into the scene brings forward another lesson and another alignment of contrasts. The authorities and their allies are fated from the beginning of the Gospel to be opponents of Jesus because they stand for disbelief and untruth—synonymous realities in the symbolic world of John's Gospel.[19] However, the Fourth Gospel is not cast in purely dualistic categories. Truth has a public character in John's perspective. Those who "love darkness" and whose "deeds are evil" shun the light and seek darkness less they be exposed; this is the role of the opponents (3:19-20). But there are others who have an affinity for the light and strive to do "what is true."

These "come to the light" (3:21). Jesus' mission, in Johannine terms, is to "come as light into the world, so that everyone who believes in me should not remain in the darkness" (12:46).

While many of the characters in the Gospel play fixed roles of "light" or "darkness," some, such as Peter, illustrate movement from darkness to light. The Passion story displays the struggle of discipleship.[20] Under the threat of exposure and even death, Peter succombs to fear and falls back into the darkness. But Peter has been called into the light by Jesus and that call will not be thwarted, even by the power of darkness. Peter's desperate longing to follow Jesus even to death is repeated in the Gospel (see 6:68; 13:37) and the final chapter implies that the apostle would ultimately give his life in witness to his discipleship (see 21:18-19).

But for now, in the crisis of the Passion, the reader is left to ponder varying responses to Jesus, some purely hostile and some painfully weak.

[19] See above, pp. 39–40.

[20] As does the figures of Joseph of Arimathea and particularly Nicodemus in the burial story (19:38-42) see the discussion of this theme, below, pp. 159-163.

III. Jesus on Trial (18:28-19:16)

Introduction

The trial of Jesus before Pilate is the longest and most intricately crafted scene of John's Passion narrative. Typical themes, already breaking the surface in the previous incidents of the Passion story, come into full view here. Through deft use of irony, the evangelist proclaims Jesus as King of the Jews and Son of God. Jesus' mission is again boldly stated: he is the revealer of ultimate truth to the world. By giving his life out of love for the world, Jesus triumphs over evil and death. And all who encounter Jesus must ultimately choose to acknowledge the truth or be consumed by falsehood.

These vigorous Johannine themes are proclaimed in the most unlikely of settings. Jesus is a prisoner, denounced by the religious leaders of his own people, abandoned and denied by his own disciples, and standing bound before the summit of secular power. The evangelist savors the irony of this scene: in a setting of abject weakness, Jesus is transparently powerful.

THE LITERARY DESIGN OF THE TRIAL SCENE

John uses a "split screen" to achieve his dramatic effect. The trial takes place at the "praetorium" (19:28), the temporary residence of the Roman Prefect while in Jerusalem. The setting shifts back and forth, from inside the praetorium where Pilate and Jesus are sequestered to the turbulent agitation of the Jewish leaders who remain outside.

The end result is a chain of seven brief episodes, alternating between the "inside" and "outside" locations:

(1) "outside"—The Jewish leaders hand Jesus over to Pilate for condemnation, 18:28-32;

(2) "inside"—Pilate interrogates Jesus about his kingship, 18:33-38a;

(3) "outside"—Pilate declares Jesus innocent, 18:38b-40;

(4) "inside"—The Roman soldiers scourge and mock Jesus, 19:1-3;

(5) "outside"—Pilate again declares Jesus not guilty, 19:4-8;
(6) "inside"—Pilate interrogates Jesus about his origin, 19:9-12;
(7) "outside"—Pilate delivers Jesus to crucifixion, 19:13-16.
Some authors suggest that the evangelist deliberately designed
a "chaiastic" relationship among the scenes with the 1st and 7th
scene, the 2nd and 4th, and the 3rd and 5th centering on related
themes. The scourging and mocking of Jesus for his claims to
kingship would be the unparalled middle scene that presents in
vivid, even wrenching terms, the ultimate issues of the trial: the
one who is mocked for royal pretensions is, in fact, the true king.[1]

While the evangelist's careful and artful construction of this
scene is clear, the attempt to pin down the details of its design
can be overplayed. The evangelist obviously uses the alternation
of "inside" and "outside" settings to organize the scene and to
achieve much of its dramatic impact. But this division is not
pressed in an absolutely consistent way. For example, explicit
reference to going "inside" is missing at the beginning of the
scourging scene (19:1) and in 19:12 the Jews who are "outside"
seem to be present for the "inside" interrogation of Jesus by Pilate. And though the chaiastic parallels between the various scenes
are quite convincing, they should not be overemphasized. The
scourging and mocking of Jesus—the centerpiece of the chaiastic pattern—is not, in fact, the dramatic summit of the trial.

The power of the trial scene is found not in the symmetry of
its structure but in the dynamism of the narrative. The drama in-
tensifies as it moves from the initial confrontation between Pilate and the Jewish leaders through to the final demands for Jesus'
crucifixion and Pilate's reluctant deliverance of Jesus to death.
Several strands work their way through the scene and contribute
to the mounting emotion of the trial: the behavior of each of the
main characters—Pilate, the Jewish leaders, and Jesus—and the
staging of the scene from start to finish.

Pilate, for example, begins with seemingly cool insolence when
first presented with the leaders' demands and in his subsequent
interrogation of Jesus. But when his initial declaration of Jesus'
innocence is violently rebuffed by the "Jews," the prefect himself is drawn into the struggle: first attempting to release Jesus

---

[1] This analysis is provided in R. Brown, *The Gospel According to John XIII-XXI*, 858–59.

according to the Passover custom; then in a crude and twisted ploy, having the prisoner scourged to demonstrate his innocence; then gripped with fear as he senses the mysterious nature of Jesus; and finally trying one last desperate attempt to have Jesus released by presenting him to the Jews as their king.

The evangelist also portrays the behavior of the Jewish leaders as becoming more intense and more desperate as the trial moves to its climax. They spar with Pilate over legalities in the opening scene but their determination to condemn Jesus becomes fiercer as the trial progresses: first choosing Barabbas over Jesus; then demanding the crucifixion of the scourged and humiliated prisoner Pilate presents to them; and, finally, seeming to lose their very identity as they claim allegiance only to Caesar rather than acknowledge Jesus as king.

With exceptional skill, the evangelist meanwhile portrays Jesus himself calmly asserting his majesty while hostility and desperation swirl around him. Jesus does not speak to the Jewish authorities; his last word to them was at the interrogation by Annas (18:23). The authorities are portrayed by John as having lost their ear for the truth; there is nothing more that Jesus can say to them. But he does speak to Pilate, firmly declaring the nature of his kingship, and identifying the source of his own authority while reminding the prefect of the limits on his. When Pilate's indifference to the truth becomes apparent, Jesus ceases to speak to him as well.

The "inside"—"outside" staging of the trial supports all of these dramatic movements in the scene. The frantic shuttling of Pilate from inside to outside seems to accelerate as the resistance of the leaders' becomes more fierce and the mysterious power of Jesus more evident. The reader moves with Pilate from one location to the other: hearing the revealing words of Jesus in the privacy of the praetorium counterpointed by the fury of the crowd whenever the action steps outside. The barriers between inside and outside seem to dissolve in the final scene where the demands of the Jewish leaders that Jesus be condemned break into Pilate's consciousness as he is "inside" with Jesus (19:12).

Pilate's presentations to the crowd also escalate: first he comes out to learn what is their demands (18:29); then he declares that Jesus is innocent (18:38b), next he brings with him the scourged and battered prisoner (19:4); and, finally, he emerges to take his place on the judgment seat, and presents Jesus to the crowd as their king.

The terse concluding verse—"then he handed him over to them to be crucified"—abruptly and effectively closes down the burning drama of the entire scene.

The relationship of John's account of the trial to that of the Synoptic Gospels remains an intriguing mystery. Similar to the other Gospels, John makes Jesus' identity as king the central issue of the Roman trial.[2] John also agrees in making the chief protagonists in the trial the Jewish leaders on the one hand and Pontius Pilate, the Roman prefect, on the other. In his usual fashion, John tends to merge the leadership groups into one designation, "the Jews," while the Synoptics refer to specific factions among the leaders.[3] The Synoptic Gospels also give a role to the "crowds," an element missing in John's narrative.[4]

But the overall cast of the trial scene in John's Gospel is unique and is clearly the product of the evangelist's literary skill and theological perspective. The evangelist may have been acquainted with the Synoptic versions of the trial or was in touch with other well shaped traditions about a climactic trial before the Roman prefect. But no matter what his sources may have been, John leaves his own dramatic stamp on this key scene of the Passion narrative.

[28] Then they took Jesus from Caiaphas to Pilate's headquarters. It was early in the morning. They themselves did not

---

[2] Mark's presentation of the Roman trial sets the pattern for this (Mk 15:1-20); see D. Senior, *The Passion of Jesus in the Gospel of Mark*, 105–14. The importance of the kingship motif in John is stressed by D. Rensberger, *Johannine Faith and Liberating Community (Philadelphia: Westminster, 1988), 70–106, 116–180; see also, B. D. Ehrman, "Jesus' Trial Before Pilate: John 18:28–19:16," Biblical Theology Bulletin* 13 (1983), 124–31; V. Pfitzner, "The Coronation of the King—Passion Narrative and Passion Theology in the Gospel of St. John," *Lutheran Theological Journal* 10 (1976), 1–12; C. H. Giblin, "John's Narration at the Hearing Before Pilate," *Biblica* 67 (1986) 221–39.

[3] On some of the negative implications of this for contemporary interpretation of the Gospel, see below, pp. 155–57.

[4] See, however, Matthew 27:14-25 where leaders and people merge into "the whole people." On the meaning of this text, see D. Senior, *The Passion of Jesus in the Gospel of Matthew*, 116–22.

enter the headquarters, so as to avoid ritual defilement and to be able to eat the Passover. [29] So Pilate went out to them and said, "What accusation do you bring against this man?" [30] They answered, "If this man were not a criminal, we would not have handed him over to you." [31] Pilate said to them, "Take him yourselves and judge him according to your law." The Jews replied, "We are not permitted to put anyone to death." [32] (This was to fulfil what Jesus had said when he indicated the kind of death he was to die.)

[33] Then Pilate entered the headquarters again, summoned Jesus, and asked him, "Are you the King of the Jews?" [34] Jesus answered, "Do you ask this on your own, or did others tell you about me?" [35] Pilate replied, "I am not a Jew, am I? Your own nation and the chief priests have handed you over to me. What have you done?" [36] Jesus answered, "My kingdom is not from this world; if my kingdom were from this world, my followers would be fighting to keep me from being handed over to the Jews. But as it is, my kingdom is not from here." [37] Pilate asked him, "So you are a king?" Jesus answered, "You say that I am a king. For this I was born, and for this I came into the world, to testify to the truth. Everyone who belongs to the truth listens to my voice." [38a] Pilate asked him, "What is truth?"

[38b] After he had said this, he went out to the Jews again and told them, "I find no case against him.[39] But you have a custom that I release someone for you at the Passover. Do you want me to release for you the King of the Jews?" [40] They shouted in reply, "Not this man, but Barabbas!" Now Barabbas was a bandit.

[1] Then Pilate took Jesus and had him flogged. [2] And the soldiers wove a crown of thorns and put it on his head, and they dressed him in a purple robe. [3] They kept coming up to him, saying, "Hail, King of the Jews!" and striking him on the face.

[4] Pilate went out again, and said to them, "Look, I am bringing him out to you to let you know that I find no case against him." [5] So Jesus came out, wearing the crown of thorns and the purple robe. Pilate said to them, "Here is the man!" [6] When the chief priests and the police saw him, they

shouted, "Crucify him! Crucify him!" Pilate said to them, "Take him yourselves and crucify him; I find no case against him." [7] The Jews answered him, "We have a law, and according to that law he ought to die because he has claimed to be the Son of God." [8] Now when Pilate heard this, he was more afraid than ever.

[9] He entered his headquarters again and asked Jesus, "Where are you from?" But Jesus gave him no answer. [10] Pilate therefore said to him, "Do you refuse to speak to me? Do you not know that I have power to release you, and power to crucify you? [11] Jesus answered him, "You would have no power over me unless it had been given you from above; therefore the one who handed me over to you is guilty of a greater sin." [12] From then on Pilate tried to release him, but the Jews cried out, "If you release this man, you are no friend of the emperor. Everyone who claims to be a king sets himself against Caesar the emperor."

[13] When Pilate heard these words, he brought Jesus outside and sat on the judge's bench at a place called The Stone Pavement, or in Hebrew, Gabbatha. [14] Now it was the day of Preparation for the Passover; and it was about noon. He said to the Jews, "Here is your King!" [15] They cried out, "Away with him! Away with him! Crucify him!" Pilate asked them, "Shall I crucify your King?" The chief priests answered, "We have no king but the emperor." [16] Then he handed him over to them to be crucified.

a) *The Jewish Leaders hand Jesus over to Pilate for condemnation (18:28-32).*

The first episode of the trial scene picks up the narrative after Peter's denial (18:25-27). At dawn, Jesus is led from the "house of Caiaphas" to the praetorium where the Jewish leaders will deliver him to Pilate.

There are a number of gaps left in John's account. In 18:24 John had noted that Jesus was sent bound to Caiaphas, but there is no report on what happened there. And Pilate is brought into the drama without any introduction (18:29), the evangelist seeming to presume the readers' knowledge that this was the Roman prefect. Nor is the reader given any briefing on the nature of the accusations leveled at Jesus. Even though Pilate asks the Jewish leaders what accusations they have against Jesus (18:29), as the trial progresses Pilate already seems to know about Jesus' supposed claims to kingship (18:33).

There are also some baffling historical issues raised by this opening episode. The location of the "praetorium" or "headquarters" is debated. The Roman prefect who ruled over the districts of Judea and Samaria normally resided in Caesarea, a Herodian city on the Mediterranean coast, but from time to time would come to visit Jerusalem. Some have suggested he would stay at the Antonium fortress adjacent to the northern wall of the Temple. A garrison of Roman soldiers was stationed in this strategic location to insure order, especially during the feastdays when up to a hundred thousand pilgrims would nearly double the population of Jerusalem. Another possible location, however, would be Herod's palace on the southwestern heights of the city. A growing number of historians favor this location since the palatial setting of Herod's place would be a more likely residence for the Roman ruler than the barracks atmosphere of the Antonium.[5]

Reference to the Passover also raises a significant historical question about the Johannine chronology compared to that of the other Gospels. In the Synoptics, Jesus dies on the feast of Passover itself (see Mk 14:12 and parallels), with the last supper being presented as a Passover meal, beginning in the normal Jewish fashion after sundown of the evening before. But in John's account the Friday on which Jesus dies is the *eve* of Passover, with the sabbath coinciding with the Passover feast. Therefore the final meal with the disciples which took place the day before the eve of the feast could not be a Passover meal and John does not attempt to describe it as such.

Various attempts have been made to reconcile the two chronologies, including the suggestion that John's Gospel may be following a different liturgical calendar in the manner of the Qumran community.[6] Some argument could be made that John's chro-

---

[5] See, J. Wilkinson, *Jerusalem as Jesus Knew It* (London: Thames and Hudson, 1978), 137–42.

[6] See the work of A. Jaubert, *The Date of the Last Supper* (Staten Island: Alba House, 1965)

nology is more historically probable since it seems unlikely that the Jewish authorities would be involved in proceedings taking place on the feast of Passover itself. There is no satisfactory solution to this issue and, as will be pointed out below, John exploits his chronology for theological purposes—whatever the strength of the historical traditions to which he had access.

A final historical issue raised in this scene is whether or not at this period the Jewish authorities had the power of capital punishment. The statement of the leaders—"It is not lawful for us to put any man to death"—clearly implies that they did not. Historians are still divided on this issue.[7] Some argue that later rabbinic texts and the mention of public executions in the first century Jewish historian Josephus and other New Testament writers (e.g., Steven and James in Acts 7:54-60; 12:2) demonstrate that the Sanhedrin did have such authority. Others, though, arguing from general Roman administrative procedures, doubt that a Roman provincial official would delegate such an important power to the Jewish leaders.

Standing behind this historical debate is a more existential issue. Many of those who believe that the Jewish Sanhedrin did not have the power of capital punishment would interpret John's account as a later attempt to further implicate the Jewish authorities in the death of Jesus, a tendency of the New Testament writings that has fueled later Christian anti-semitism. In other words, historically the Romans were the ones who had the major responsibility for the death of Jesus, as proven by his death by crucifixion, a Roman means of public execution. In an atmosphere of hostility between the synagogue and the early Christian church, the evangelist portrayed the Jewish leaders as the initiators of the judgment against Jesus. At the same time, by downplaying Roman involvement, the evangelist would manage to ward off imperial concerns about the revolutionary tendencies of Jesus and the movement he initiated. In John's scenario the Jewish leaders them-

---

and the critique of her thesis in R. Brown, "The Date of the Last Supper," *The Bible Today* 11 (1964) 727-33.

[7] See the discussion and literature cited in D. Senior, *The Passion of Jesus in the Gospel of Mark*, 88-90: and E. Bammel, "The Trial Before Pilate" in E. Bammel and C.F.D. Moule, (eds.), *Jesus and the Politics of His Day*, 415-51.

selves wanted to condemn Jesus, but they had to turn to the Romans because they lacked the power to exercise capital punishment. This both pins responsiblity on the Jewish leaders and signals to the Roman reader of the Gospel story that Jesus was not perceived as dangerous by the Roman officials of the time. Only at the instigation of the Jewish leaders and after repeated declarations of Jesus' innocence, did Pilate reluctantly accede to their demands for crucifixion.

Solving these historical issues is practically impossible. It is true that the Gospels in general, including that of John, underscore the responsibility of the Jewish leaders for Jesus' death and, at the same time, stress that Roman authority found Jesus innocent of charges of sedition. One of the baffling theological concerns of early Christianity was to understand why Judaism had not wholeheartedly embraced the Gospel. This theological enterprise was complicated in many places by growing tension and hostility between Jews and Christians as each religious community was attempting to find its way in difficult circumstances. The Christians were trying to survive as a minority group within the Roman empire and would not want needlessly to ignite Roman suspicions about their loyalty to the state.

But to dismiss John's scenario as solely a convenient fabrication for polemic purposes against the Jews is to go too far. Likewise, one should not overstate John's benign treatment of Roman authority. John's account does not absolve Pilate of responsibility for Jesus' death nor does it ultimately portray him in positive tones.

In fact, these historical questions are generally ignored or left hanging by the evangelist because they are not at the center of his focus. He is not trying to give a comprehensive picture of the proceedings against Jesus nor to dispassionately assess the historical roles of Jews and Romans. His main point is to proclaim by means of this narrative the compelling theological message that commands the entire Passion story.[8] We can now turn to some of those concerns evident in this first episode.

---

[8] See below, Part III, on John's Passion and anti-semitism, pp. 155–57.

The Irony of Defilement

The "inside"—"outside" deployment of the trial scene begins when the Jewish leaders refuse to enter the praetorium because they fear "defilement" which would prevent them from celebrating the Passover meal that evening. Presumably such defilement or cultic impurity would be due to contact with Gentiles.[9] The irony of the leaders' decision stands out from the page. They are concerned about the proper disposition for celebrating the Passover at the very moment they deliver up to death Jesus, the "Lamb of God"!

John makes a deft use of Passover symbolism in the Passion story and this, ultimately, may be the reason for the distinctive chronology of his account discussed above.[10] As the "Book of Glory" began the evangelist noted that the feast of Passover was near. This feast of liberation signaled for Jesus that "the hour had come to depart out of this world to the Father" (see 13:1). The climax of the trial—the condemnation of Jesus—would come at the very moment the lambs were being prepared by the priests for slaughter in the Temple (19:14). And the evangelist explicitly links the fact that Jesus' legs were not broken to Passover symbolism (19:36). At the very beginning of the Gospel, the Baptist had declared that Jesus was the "Lamb of God who takes away the sins of the world" (1:29, 35).[11] Now at the beginning of the trial, John presents the Lamb, whose blood would be poured out in love for the world, standing unrecognized before his captors. It is a truly ironic moment that, for the reader, both indicts the enemies of Jesus for their failure to recognize the truth and affirms the God-given destiny of Jesus.

---

[9] The extent of cultic impurity one incurred through mere contact with a Gentile at this period is a matter of debate. There is some evidence that casual contact might simply demand immersion in a bath to restore purity. But contact with a corpse caused more serious contamination, as legislated in Numbers 9:7-12, and would mean seven days of purification. Celebration of the Passover for those so contaminated would have to put off to the following month. Some later rabbinic texts refer to the fear of such contamination by entering a Gentile home since they had the custom of burying the dead in the house. See, R. Brown, *The Gospel According to John XIII-XXI*, 845–46.

[10] See above, pp. 74-75.

[11] See above, Part I, pp. 33-34.

The exchange between Pilate and the Jewish leaders is caustic. When the Prefect asks the nature of the charge, the leaders seem to deliberately provoke him: "If this man were not a criminal, we would not have handed him over" (18:30). Pilate retorts in the same spirit, challenging the leaders to "take him yourselves and judge him by your law" (18:31). Finally, the leaders concede that they do not have the power to do what they need to do: "We are not permitted to put any one to death" (18:32).

On one level this exchange could be read as a typical, teeth-clenched exchange between parties who despise each other but upon whom circumstances force a degree of collaboration. But the fact that the evangelist sees this first dialogue of the trial as fufilling Jesus' word about the manner of death he was to die (18:32) signals that a deeper purpose than dramatic tension is intended. Johannine irony is again at work. The leaders brand Jesus "a criminal" (18:30)—the reader knows the incredible untruth of so naming one whom the Gospel describes as "doing the works of God" (5:36). The fact that the leaders must come to Pilate because of legal technicalities also has the ironic effect of drawing out what the evangelist has described throughout the Gospel as their true intentions. Early in Jesus' ministry they had resolved to kill him because of his claims to be doing the works of God and to be God's Son (5:18; 7:1, 19, 25; 8:59; 10:31; 11:53).[12] Now those hostile intentions are unmasked. On their own lips they identify themselves as the ones who "hand over" Jesus to death (see below, 19:11).

Above all, this exchange between Pilate and the leaders signals that Jesus' God-given mission is moving inexorably to its completion. The reader has known all along, because of Jesus' own prophetic words, that being "lifted up" on the cross would be the final act.[13] It was not, ultimately, the success of the leaders' plot to snare Jesus nor the brutal power of Rome to inflict crucifixion that wrote this script. In Jerusalem shortly before the feast Jesus had declared the truth that only now the leaders were forced to admit:

---

[12] See above, Part I, pp. 39–40.
[13] See above, pp. 34–36.

" 'Now is the judgment of this world; now the ruler of this world be driven out. And I, when I am lifted up from the earth, will draw all people to myself.' He said this to indicate the kind of death he was to die." (12:31-33)

Once again John portrays Jesus as sovereignly free in moments of apparent subjection. No one takes Jesus' life from him, he lays it down of his own free will (10:17-18).

b) *Pilate interrogates Jesus about his Kingship (18:33-38a).*
After hearing the leaders' demands, Pilate goes back inside the Praetorium for his first conversation with Jesus. This episode introduces the motif of Jesus' kingship, a fundamental theological symbol that sets the tone for the entire trial.

Pilate's question—"Are you the King of the Jews?" (18:33)—comes without preparation for the reader. Pilate, the representative of Roman imperial power, evokes the symbol of kingship, a symbol where truth and untruth, love and hatred, God and the world will clash. Fears about Jesus' claims to political power were undoubtedly part of the historical forces that brought him to his death.[1] But John's interests in the Passion story are theological: the symbol that represents the summit of political power enables the evangelist to reveal the true nature of Jesus and his mission.

Jesus' first response to Pilate begins to drive a wedge between the surface, purely political meaning of the symbol and its deeper theological significance. Jesus does not immediately answer Pilate's question but poses one of his own: the prisoner interrogates his interrogator! Pilate is pressed for his own statement of the truth: "Do you ask this on your own, or did others tell you about me?" (18:34).

The reader can find in Pilate's retort—"I am not a Jew, am I? Your own nation and the chief priests have handed you over to me. What have you done?" (18:35)—multiple layers of meaning, a characteristic of John's literary style. Pilate confirms the hostile intent of the Jewish leaders: they, indeed, are the ones who have

---

[1] See the discussion in D. Rengsburger, *Johannine Faith and Liberating Community*, 87–90 and R. Horsley, *Sociology and the Jesus Movement*. (New York: Crossroad, 1990), 130–45.

"handed over" Jesus (see 18:30; 19:11).[2] But he also asks an open-ended question—"what have you done?"—that enables the Gospel to reflect on the totality of Jesus' mission to the world. The reader knows that what Jesus "has done" are not crimes deserving punishment but acts of redeeming love that will climax with his death on the cross.

Jesus' declaration moves the conversation in this direction: "My kingdom is not from this world; if my kingdom were from this world, my followers would be fighting to keep me from being handed over to the Jews. But my kingdom is not from here" (18:36). These words are saturated with Johannine theology and can be properly understood only from that perspective.

In the Synoptic Gospels the metaphor of the "Kingdom" or "Rule of God" plays a major role, in contrast to John's Gospel were it is used sparingly.[3] John refers only twice to the "Kingdom of God" (3:3, 5) but does portray Jesus as a royal figure whose enrthonement on the cross insures God's sovereignty over the world. In the Synoptic Gospels the metaphor is played out in a temporal framework. The full establishment of the rule of God is a *future* event, but that future reality begins to impinge on the present through the words and actions of Jesus. Jesus' acts of healing and exorcism, for example, bring the liberating experience of God's rule to those who experience them (see Mt. 12:28; Luke 11:20).

But John's Gospel often prefers to cast the contrasting realities of a sinful present and a redeemed future into *spatial,* rather than temporal, terms. God's realm where truth and love abide is "above"; it is another "world." The sphere in which darkness, untruth, and hatred exercise their toxic power is "below," in "this world." The modern reader should not confuse John's categories with the traditional distinction between "heaven" and "earth," thereby driving a wedge between an "earthly kingdom" involving the here and now gritty world of political, economic and so-

---

[2] Note that here the evangelist singles out the "chief priests" as leading the opposition to Jesus: see also 7:32, 45; 11:47, 49–53, 57; 12:10. "Nation" as a comprehensive designation for the Jews is found in 11:48, 50, 51, 52.

[3] See B. Viviano, *The Kingdom of God in History* (Good News Studies 27; Wilmington: Michael Glazier, 1988), 13–29.

cial realities and a future "heavenly kingdom" above and beyond such realities. John's perspective is quite different. The evangelist portrays two co-existing and yet ultimately conflicting "worlds" of values and meaning. One is a deadly "world" ruled by darkness and untruth and ultimately demonic; the other is God's "world" or realm, where truth and love reign. The historical human arena weaves between these two "worlds," at times capitulating to the world of evil and thus "hating" Jesus and the Gospel (15:18-19; 17:14); but at other times yearning to be free and thus the object of God's redeeming love (see 3:16-17).[4]

This Johannine perspective provides the key to the meaning of Jesus' words to Pilate. Jesus kingship is "not from this world" (18:36)—not in the sense that it is without impact on the everyday world of political power. Rather, its source of power is not "from this world"—namely, not defined by or finding its source of power in the same world of values that Pilate and the Jewish leaders represent.[5] If Jesus' power were from the same source as theirs then it would manifest itself in the same way that Pilate's own power and that of the religious authorities had: by the use of violence and untruth. But Jesus was not "from this world" and therefore had rejected such a course at the moment of his arrest when Peter had taken up the sword against Malchus (see 18:11).

Thus John's Gospel, along with the Synoptics, uses the incident of Jesus' arrest by armed captors to reflect on the incompatibilty between the spirit of the Gospel and the use of violence.[6]

Pilate restates his initial question, perhaps intended in mocking tones: "So you are a king?." In characteristic Johannine language, the question leads to the Gospel's most powerful statement of Jesus' royal mission:

[4] See above, pp. 16–18.

[5] See D. Hill, "My Kingdom is not of this world (Jn 18:36)—Conflict and Christian Existence in the World According to the Fourth Gospel," *Irish Biblical Studies* 9 (1987) 54–62; D. Rensberger, *Johannine Faith and Liberating Community,* 97–98; R. Baum-Bodenbender, *Hoheit in Niedrigkeit.* Johanneische Christologie im Prozess Jesu vor Pilatus (Joh 18:18–19:16a) (Forschung zur Bibel, 49; Wurzburg: Echter, 1984).

[6] See D. Senior, "The New Testament and Peacemaking: Some Problem Passages," *Faith and Mission* 4 (1987) 71–77; J.A.T. Robinson, "His Witness is True," in E. Bammel and C.F.D. Moule (eds.), *Jesus and the Politics of His Day,* 453–76.

"You say that I am a king. For this I was born, and for this
I came into the world, to testify to the truth. Everyone who
belongs to the truth listens to my voice." (18:37)

Jesus subtly confirms that Pilate himself has stated the truth
he seems to resist: "You say that I am a king."[7] To be a "king"
is the very purpose of Jesus' mission in the world. That God-given
sovereignty is expressed not in oppressive force but in "bear(ing)
witness to the truth." Bearing witness to the truth is a fundamental
theme of John's Gospel and one already evoked in Jesus' response
during his interrogation by Annas (see 18:19-23). Jesus *is* the
"Truth"; to know him is to know God (14:6). The theme of truth
and its acceptance or rejection had dominated Jesus' conflict with
the Jewish leaders in chapter 8.[8] As the "light of the world" Jesus
came that those who follow him might have "the light of life"
(8:12). But the leaders accuse him of bearing false testimony (8:13)
and of being in league with Satan (8:48).

Much of the rest of chapter 8 is taken up with Jesus' defense
of his mission of truth. Jesus' testimony is ultimately that he is
sent from God to save the world. Those who are in tune with the
truth are able to recognize Jesus as the genuine revealer of God
and to trust his message. But those whose lives cling to falsehood
cannot hear his voice and reject him. "Whoever is from God hears
the words of God. The reason you do not hear them is that you
are not from God" (8:47). The sharp polemical tone of chapter
8 accuses the leaders of being demonic in inspiration: "Why do
you not understand what I say? It is because you cannot accept
my word. You are from your father the devil, and you choose
to do your father's desires. He was a murderer from the beginning, and does not stand in the truth, because there is no truth
in him" (8:43-44).

The theme of truth and falsehood in this earlier chapter of
John's Gospel not only identifies Jesus' mission as the revelation
of God's truth to the world—a truth ultimately demonstrated in
Jesus' death—but it also provides the fundamental explanation
for the rejection of Jesus. The leaders whose resistance to Jesus

---

[7] This is similar to sense of Jesus' reply to Caiaphas in Mt 26:64 and to Pilate in 27:11.

[8] See above, pp. 60–63; also, 3:31-16.

is unyielding are acting in accord with their nature which is immersed in falsehood and has its source in the spirit of evil. The final demonstration of this is in the Passion.

This episode of the trial closes with Pilate's famous question: "What is truth?" (18:38a). Apart from their immediate context in the Passion story these words can be interpreted as an expression of cool and worldly cynicism, or as agnostic futility in the search for lasting truth. But following on Jesus' words about the meaning of truth and the Gospel's portrayal of Jesus himself as the Truth sent from God to illumine the world, Pilate's words are self-condemning.[9] He joins ranks with the religious leaders; he cannot understand Jesus or his words because he is "not from God" (8:47). "Judgement" in Johannine theology is not a trial conducted by God but self-judgment brought on by refusing to be open to the truth.[10] The Johannine Gospel does not exonerate Pilate or attempt to curry favor with Roman authorities; on the contrary, it condemns Pilate and his power as blind to the truth and mired in falsehood.

c) *Pilate Declares Jesus Innocent (18:38b-40)*

A new episode begins as Pilate goes outside to declare Jesus innocent. Pilate attempts a ploy to placate the Jewish authorities. He reminds them of their custom of having a prisoner released on the occasion of the Passover and suggests that the choice be "the King of the Jews" (18:39). But they refuse: "Not this man, but Barabbas!" (18:40).

The scene is drenched with Johannine irony. A Gentile official finds Jesus innocent while the Jewish leaders stand firm in their rejection of him. This is a foretaste of the ultimate failure of the early community's mission to Israel and the corresponding growth of the Gentile churches. This historical and theological paradox is a deep current of John's Gospel, and, indeed, of the entire New Testament, and John brings it strongly to the fore here.[11] In Mark

---

[9] See A. Dauer, *Die Passionsgeschichte im Johannesevangelium* (STANT 30; München: Kösel, 1972), 253-62; I. de la Potterie, *The Hour of Jesus,* 68-74.

[10] See 3:18-21; 12:44-50.

[11] We cannot forget that most of the earliest generation of Christians were Jewish in origin, and Hellenistic Judaism was influential in the success of the Gentile mission. But by the end

(15:8) and Luke (23:18) the *crowd* takes the initiative in reminding the prefect of the Passover custom, but in John's version Pilate himself introduces this way of releasing Jesus.[12]

The depth of the leaders' blindness is confirmed by the ironic
fact that they choose over Jesus a man whom John labels as a
"bandit" (18:40 the Greek word is *leistes,* meaning "robber" or
"brigand"). Jesus had called the Jewish leaders themselves
"thieves and robbers" *(leistes)* because they were false shepherds
(10:1, 8). Now these same leaders choose such a man in the place
of Jesus.[13] At the last supper, Jesus had warned that the "world
would love you as its own" and would hate the disciples as it had
hated Jesus (15:18). That alliance of untruth and violence was
now being demonstrated in the Passion.

d) *The Roman Soldiers Scourge and Mock Jesus (19:1-3).*

This cruel and poignant episode stands at the center of the chais-
tic pattern John imposes on the Trial scene. John's placement of
the scene here in the middle of the trial does not coincide with
the Synoptic versions. In Mark and Matthew the scourging (and
its accompanying mockery) takes place after the condemnation
of Jesus and immediately before his execution (see Mk 15:17-20;
Mt 27:28-31). In Luke's account Pilate threatens scourging as a
punishment (Lk 23:22) but apparently does not carry it out once
Jesus is condemned to crucifixion.[14] The Synoptic versions, in fact,
have more historical plausibility. Flogging was used by the
Romans as either as a prelude for capital punishment or as a form

---

of the first century and in the wake of the Jewish revolt—the vantage point of John—the
Church was predominantly Gentile and there was lingering hostility with the synagogue. See
a discussion of this evolution in B. Meyer, *The Early Christians: Their World Mission &
Self-Discovery* (Good News Studies 16; Wilmington: Michael Glazier, 1986) and J.
Charlesworth (ed.), *Jews and Christians* (New York: Crossroad, 1990), particularly the es-
say by D. Smith, "Judaism and the Gospel of John," 76-99.

[12] There is no available historical evidence for this custom outside of the Gospels; it could
well have been a local custom introduced to coincide with the celebration of Passover; see,
C. K. Barrett, *The Gospel According to St. John,* 538.

[13] See B. Lindars, *The Gospel of John,* 563;

[14] Note that the mockery by Herod and the taunting by the prisoners may be something of
a substitute for these scenes in Luke; see D. Senior, *The Passion of Jesus in the Gospel of
Luke,* 112-18.

of punishment in itself.[15] There is no evidence of its being used in the midst of a trial as in John's account.

John's purposes are clearly dramatic and theological. The cruelty inflicted on Jesus prepares for the subsequent episode when the battered prisoner will be brought out and displayed to the crowd (19:4). More importantly, it adds further depth and force to John's ironic perspective on kingship.

Jesus is mocked by the Roman soldiers for his pretensions to kingship (19:2-3). The major symbols of royal power are conferred on him, but in each case with viscious mockery so that Jesus' claim to royal status is ridiculed and denied. He is crowned, but with a crown of thorns. He is given a purple robe and hailed as "King of the Jews!" by the soldiers, but blows rather than acts of respect punctuate their homage.

The reader, of course, knows that Jesus *is* a "king" and that through him the divine source of all genuine power is revealed. From the perspective of the Gospel, therefore, the mockery turns back upon itself. It is not Jesus who is derided in this scene but the trappings of human sovereignty: the crown, the royal robe, the acclamations and rituals of homage. True dignity and power are now expressed in the anti-signs of seeming powerlessness born by this prisoner. John will continue this manner of discourse in the scenes that follow: the presentations of the King Jesus to the crowds and his "enthronement" on the cross. Through irony John's Gospel is able to be seditious.

The surface motives for Pilate's decision to so humiliate Jesus are not clear: Is it intended to win the sympathy of the crowd? Or is it an assertion of Pilate's power in the face of a challenge to imperial authority, no matter how ludicrous is the source of that challenge? John's account does not answer these questions. But the fact that Pilate orders Jesus' scourging (19:1) can only be read as a terrible sin in a narrative that presents Jesus as the Word of God. Pilate's action—whether a brazen exercise of power or a cynical and cowardly ploy—once again demonstrates the Gospel's negative portrayal of one who cannot recognize the truth and therefore whose acts become lies.[16] His next fateful step is to deliver Jesus to death.

[15] R. Brown, *The Gospel According to John XIII-XXI*, 814.

[16] See R. Schnackenburg, *The Gospel According to St. John*, Vol. 3, 253–54; R. Kysar, *John*, 285.

e) *Pilate Presents Jesus to the Leaders and Again Declares His Innocence (19:4-8)*

With this episode the dramatic tension of the trial sharply escalates. Pilate goes outside to the Jewish leaders and announces that he is going to present Jesus to them to declare again his innocence. But when the battered prisoner emerges in full view of the crowd, the ploy fails. The leaders demand that Jesus be crucified because he has claimed to be the "Son of God" and thus deserves death under Jewish law.

While the scene continues the motif of kingship that dominated the previous episodes and has a certain parallel to Pilate's first declaration of Jesus' innocence (see 18:38b-40), the public presentation of Jesus and the reference to his claim to be "the Son of God" are new elements which move the trial towards its climax. As before, the evangelist skillfully uses both dramatic staging and the device of irony to give the scene its force.

Pilate firmly declares Jesus' innocence (19:4) and apparently hopes that the public presentation of the scourged and abused prisoner will placate the crowd and end the matter (19:5). The public presentation may also be intended to continue the mock ritual that took place inside with the soldiers. Jesus the pretender king had received the mock symbols of power and the brutal "homage" of his retinue—now he would be presented for the "acclamation" of his subjects.

Pilate presents Jesus with words that have also taken on a life of their own in Christian art and imagination: "Here is the man!" (19:5). The *"Ecce Homo"*—Jesus standing before the crowds, crowned with thorns, at once a compelling and heart-rending royal presence—has become an icon etched in Christian memory. There is little doubt that the evangelist intended this kind of dramatic effect. But interpreters have debated whether the Johannine context of this episode gives Pilate's words another level of meaning as well. Are they to be understood merely as Pilate's expression of pity or even contempt for Jesus: i.e., "behold this pitiful human being who is not worth being the object of your hatred or my concern and should, therefore, be released"? Or does the evangelist use Pilate's words to also affirm something else about Jesus?

For some, the designation "Here is *the man*" is intended to evoke one of the Gospel's major titles for Jesus, namely that he is *"the* Man," i.e., the "Son of Man."[1] The Aramaic idiom behind this title—*Bar Nasha*—means literally, the "man" or "human being" in the generic sense and can be translated as "Son of humanity."

There is an ongoing debate about the precise meaning of this enigmatic phrase for Jesus in the Gospels. In the Synoptic Gospels it is consistently used on the lips of Jesus as a self-designation. Scholars debate whether in such Gospel texts it is used with the literal sense (i.e., this "human being") or whether it had already taken on a special titular meaning in Jewish and Christian interpretation. The same phrase is found, for example, in the Book of Daniel (7:13-14) where it refers to the renewed and triumphant Israel appearing "like a son of man" at the end of the world. Many scholars believe that in similar fashion, Christian circles used this title to refer to the exalted Christ who would return in triumph at the end of time.[2] Mark's Gospel also employs the "Son of Man" title in contexts which speak of the suffering of Jesus so that the title takes on a paradoxical sense: the "Son of Man" must suffer but will also come in triumph and exaltation at the end of the world.

In John's Gospel, too, the "Son of Man" title can refer both to the mysterious origin of Jesus who "descends" from heaven for his mission, and his "lifting up" or exaltation on the cross by which he returns to God.[3] Jesus' words to Nicodemus capture both dimensions of the title:

"No one has ascended into heaven except the one who descended from heaven, the Son of Man. And just as Moses lifted up the serpent in the wilderness, so must the Son of Man be lifted up, that whoever believes in him may have eternal life." (3:13-14; see also 6:62).

When Pilate says of Jesus—"Behold the Man!"—did the evangelist want the reader to remember this mysterious identity of Jesus

---

[1] See, for example, I. de la Potterie, *The Hour of Jesus,* 79–80; A. Dauer, *Die Passionsgeschichte,* 264–65; B. Lindars, *The Gospel of John,* 566.

[2] See the discussion in J. Dunn, *Christology in the Making* (Philadelphia: Westminster, 1980), 65–97; B. Lindars, *Jesus, Son of Man* (Grand Rapids: Eerdmans, 1983).

[3] On Son of Man in John, see the literature cited above, n. 2.

as Son of Man? Does the Roman prefect unwittingly proclaim what Jesus had predicted throughout the Gospel—that through his "lifting up" in crucifixion this son of humanity and child of God would complete his work and draw all things to himself (see 8:28; 12:31-34)?

Some interpreters prefer other possible reference points. Zechariah 6:11-12 speaks of the crowning of "Josiah" (or "Jesus") as a messianic royal figure:

> "Take the silver and gold, and make a crown, and set it on the head of the high priest Joshua son of Jehozadak; say to him: "Thus says the Lord of hosts: "Here is a man whose name is the Branch: for he shall branch out in his place, and he shall build the temple of the Lord."[4]

Another candidate would be the presentation of the suffering servant figure of Isaiah 52:13-15 whose marred and battered appearance startles the nations:

> "See, my servant shall prosper; he shall be exalted and lifted up, and shall be very high. Just as there were many who were astonished at him—so marred was his appearance, beyond human semblance, and his form beyond that of mortals—so shall he startle many nations; kings shall shut their mouths because of him; for that which has not been told them they shall see, and that which they had not heard they shall contemplate."[5]

There is no way of being sure which, if any, of these deeper meanings the evangelist intended to evoke. Authors and artists work instinctively and it is possible that the Gospel writer himself may have been unsure of the connections such a powerful scene might trigger. What is clear is the basic meaning of the presentation from which all of these other suggested interpretations take their cue: Pilate presents Jesus to the world in his most humiliated and abject state—battered, abandoned, completely vul-

[4] See C. K. Barrett, *The Gospel According to St. John,* 541; R. Brown, *The Gospel According to John XIII-XXI,* 876.

[5] See J. Forestell, *The Word of the Cross,* 85.

nerable to his enemies. As Rudolph Bultmann noted in his famous commentary on this scene: "That is the man! Look at the pitiful figure! But to the mind of the Evangelist the entire paradox of the claim of Jesus is in this way fashioned into a tremendous picture . . . The declaration "the Word became flesh' has become visible in its extremest consequence."[6] The reader, who knows the identity of Jesus and therefore understands the profound irony of this scene, realizes that this "man" is truly human but also the unique Word of God.

True to the fixed role of opposition they play throughout John's drama, the Jewish leaders are not moved by Jesus' abject appearance; instead, they demand his crucifixion. There is irony here, too. For the first time in the Gospel the hideous word "crucify" is enunciated and it comes from the lips of Jesus' own people. The bitter exchange between Pilate and the leaders, reminiscent of the caustic exchange that began the trial (18:30-31), confirms that perspective. The Jews demand crucifixion but the Roman prefect tells them to "take him yourselves and crucify him, for I find no crime in him" (19:6).

The response of the leaders introduces yet another designation for Jesus: "We have a law, and according to that law he ought to die because he has claimed to be the *Son of God"* (19:7). Apparently the leaders accuse Jesus of blasphemy because of his claim to be the "Son of God." This would be in accord with the injunction of Leviticus 24:16 which commanded that anyone who "blasphemes the name of the Lord shall be put to death; the whole congregation shall stone the blasphemer. Aliens as well as citizens, when they blaspheme the Name, shall be put to death." At least three times in John's Gospel the Jews attempt to kill Jesus for this very reason (see 5:18; 8:59; 10:31-39).

The violence of their reaction highlights the importance of the "Son of God" title in Johannine christology. Just as Pilate's initial questions in the trial forced the leaders to come out in the open with their intent to destroy Jesus (see above, 18:31-32), so now his taunts draws from them the profound reason why Jesus is rejected and why he must be crucified—his claim to be the Son

---

[6] R. Bultmann, *The Gospel of John* (Philadelphia: Westminster, 1971) 659.

of God.[7] Although the Gospel uses an array of titles for Jesus, the Son of God designation catches up that primal relationship between Jesus and God that is at the heart of John's understanding of Jesus.[8] Jesus is the "Son" who abides in the Father and the Father in him. Out of love for the world God sent the Son into the world not to condemn it but to save it (3:16-17). To acclaim Jesus as "the Son of God" is to recognize the unique identity of Jesus as intimate with God and sent by God to the world. Inspiring such a confession of Jesus' true identity is the very purpose of John's narrative (see 20:30-31).

The leaders, of course, reject Jesus' claim to sonship and consider it blasphemous. But in so stating the reason for his death they ironically confirm the deepest of Gospel truths: Jesus *is* God's Son, for this very reason he has come into the world, to accomplish the Father's will of saving the world through his redemptive death.

At the mention of this mysterious new note in the accusations, Pilate becomes "more afraid" (19:8). His "fear" is the kind of shuddering awe frequently provoked by an encounter with the transcendent in the biblical saga. Pilate's control of the situation becomes more tenuous as he begins to realize he is a player in a cosmic drama that far exceeds his comprehension or spiritual capacity.

f) *Pilate Interrogates Jesus about His Origin (19:9-12).*

Pilate and Jesus move back inside the praetorium for the next episode. The parallels are striking between this scene and the second segment of the trial narrative (18:33-38) where Pilate had questioned Jesus about the nature of his kingship. In this episode the issue is the nature of Jesus' "power."

The fearful mood of the previous scene lingers. Pilate asks this mysterious man: "Where are you from?" (19:9), the kind of open-ended, haunting question favored in John's Gospel.[9] The specific

---

[7] See R. Schnackenburg, *The Gospel According to St. John,* Vol. 3, 259.

[8] On the use of the "Son" designation in John, see R. Scroggs, *Christology in Paul and John* (Proclamation Commentaries: Philadelphia: Fortress, 1988), 67–72. Son of God is used in a confessional context.

[9] See, for example, similar questions in 1:38, 7:27-28; 8:14; 9:26-27; see further, G. Nichol-

point of the question—Jesus' origin—taps a recurrent Johannine theme. Jesus is the incarnate Word who comes forth from God and is sent into the world to reveal God's redemptive love for the world. This fundamental truth stands at the core of John's theology.[10] Recognizing Jesus' "origin" is, in Johannine perspective, the sign of authentic faith (17:8). Conversely, not to recognize "where Jesus is from" is tantamount to not recognizing or believing in Jesus.[11] In his teaching in the Temple Jesus had sharply challenged the Jewish authorities when they claimed to know where Jesus came from: "You know me, and you know where I come from? I have not come on my own. But the one who sent me is true, and you do not know him. I know him, because I am from him, and he sent me." (7:28-29). This same accusation reappears in chapter 8 when the Pharisees charge Jesus with bearing false testimony about himself. "Even if I testify on my own behalf, my testimony is valid because I know where I have come from and where I am going, but you do not know where I come from or where I am going." (8:14). And after Jesus has opened the eyes of the man born blind, the Pharisees again prove themselves spritually blind (9:40-41) when they declare: "We know that God has spoken to Moses, but as for this man, we do not know where he comes from." (9:29).

Just as Pilate had failed to recognize that Jesus was the Truth incarnate (18:38), so now he fails to recognize that Jesus comes from God. Jesus' silence signals that the gulf that already stood between Jesus and the religious leaders also separates Jesus and the Roman prefect. Jesus refuses to answer a question not motivated by an open spirit of faith.[12] In the Synoptic Passion narratives the silence of Jesus is massive and recalls the image of the Isaian Suffering Servant who bears insult and violence with restraint and humility.[13] John uses the motif of Jesus' silence spar-

---

son, *Death as Departure,* 54; L. Dewailly, " 'D'ou es-tu' (Jean 19:9)," *Revue Biblique* 92 (1985) 481-96.

[10] See above, Part I, pp. 16–17.

[11] G. Nicholson, *Death as Departure,* 54; J. Forestell, *The Word of the Cross,* 85.

[12] This diffidence about the spirit in which people approached Jesus is found earlier in the Gospel: e.g., 2:23-25.

[13] See, for example, Mark 14:61; 15:5; Lk 23:9.

ingly and it is a condemning silence different from that of the Servant.

Pilate is baffled and resentful that this prisoner he had attempted to defend now maintains silence: "Do you refuse to speak to me? Do you not know that I have power to release you, and power to crucify you?" (19:10). The prefect's question brings out into the open another of the underlying issues of the Passion narrative, indeed of the Gospel itself. Pilate, representative of imperial might, reminds Jesus of his *exousia,* his "power" or "authority." But Jesus immediately circumscribes that power and relocates its source, offering in effect a bold challenge to Pilate.[14] "You would have no power over me unless it had been given you from above; therefore the one who handed me over to you is guilty of a greater sin." (19:11).

Jesus' response should *not* be understood as an indirect endorsement of government authority, in the manner of Romans 13 where Paul locates the root of legitimate state authority in God.[15] The meaning of Jesus' words in John are quite different. Pilate has *no* authority at all over Jesus except that which is given to him in this moment of the Passion drama. John radically challenges the authority claims of Pilate, just as he does the religious claims of the Jewish leaders. Pilate's authority to condemn Jesus to crucifixion is, in the evangelist's perspective, not derived from his position as Roman prefect or the might of Rome that stood behind it, nor even from the divine warrant given to legitimate rulers of the State for the common good (Paul's view). Pilate is enabled to act against Jesus—as are the Jewish authorities—only because they are caught up in the God-directed drama of salvation. Because Jesus was destined to give his life in friendship love on the cross as the ultimate and unimpeachable sign of God's unconditional love for the world—for this reason and no other Pilate is given "power" over Jesus. The reader already knows,

---

[14] On the implications of this scene, see D. Rensberger, *Johannine Faith and Liberating Community,* 97–98.

[15] "Let every person be subject to the governing authorities; for there is no authority except from God, and those that exist have been instituted by God. Therefore whoever resists authority resists what God has appointed, and those who resist will incur judgment." (Romans 13:1-2).

because Jesus has so declared it, that all real *exousia,* all "power," has been invested in Jesus himself:

> "After Jesus had spoken these words, he looked up to heaven and said, "Father, the hour has come; glorify your Son so that the Son may glorify you, since you have given him authority *(exousia)* over all people, to give eternal life to all whom you have given him." (17:1-2; see also 5:27)

No human judge has "power" over the life of Jesus. This was made clear in the statement of Jesus that is so important for the entire spirit of the Johannine Passion account:

> "For this reason the Father loves me, because I lay down my life in order to take it up again. No one takes it from me, but I lay it down of my own accord. I have power *(exousia)* to lay it down, and I have power to take it up again: I have received this command from my Father." (10:17-18)

Whatever role Pilate plays in the drama of Jesus' death is given him "from above"—from the God who sent the Son into the world. Beyond that carefully defined perimeter, Pilate and the claims he represents have no power at all over Jesus.

Because Pilate is in reality merely a bit player on the cosmic stage, his sin is less than the one who "handed over" Jesus (19:11b). The precise referent here is not clear: is it Judas who is consistently identified as the one who "handed over" Jesus?[16] Or the High Priest who in the name of the Sanhedrin handed Jesus over to Pilate (see, for example, 18:35)? What is clear is the reaffirmation of a fundamental biblical and Johannine motif: God is the one who ultimately guides the destiny of Jesus. The crucifixion is no historical accident. In the final analysis the death of Jesus is neither the outcome of a successful plot by the Jewish leaders, nor the exercise of Pilate's imperial authority. Jesus dies because he is true to his mission of revealing God's astounding love for the world.

---

[16] See 6:71; 12:4; 13:2.

Jesus' bold declaration of power seems to shake Pilate's spirit and he resolves to set Jesus free. But Pilate's lack of faith and his inability to be open to the Truth take their toll. Those who love the darkness do evil deeds (3:19-20). The Roman prefect's lack of genuine "power" or authority becomes very evident. In a strange moment when the fierce determination of the leaders to destroy Jesus seems to penetrate the walls of the praetorium and to break down Pilate's thin resolve, John has the Jews hurl a calculated threat at the Roman prefect: "If you release this man, you are no friend of the emperor. Everyone who claims to be a king sets himself against the emperor" (19:12).

The term "friend of Ceasar" (the Greek text uses the term "Caesar") may originally have been a title of privilege for a person favored in the imperial court.[17] But in this context it is another example of biting Johannine irony. It is the Jewish leaders—not the Roman—who introduce the issue of loyalty to Caesar. And in their threat to Pilate the leaders also state a truth evident to the reader. It is true that anyone who claims to be a king challenges Caesar's power, and no greater challenge is possible than the kingship of Jesus whose God-given power eclipses by an infinite degree the pretensions of secular power.

This episode and the preceding ones, where Jesus asserted his kingship was "not from this world" and where he was mocked with the trappings of royal authority, give a "subversive" undercurrent to the trial narrative. Ultimately it is not Jesus who is on trial but those whose values and commitments are not compatible with the Gospel.

g) *Pilate delivers Jesus to Crucifixion (19:13-16).*

The commanding themes of the trial converge in this final episode: the presentation of Jesus as the true King and Passover Lamb; the rejection of Jesus by the Jewish leaders; the corruption and deception of secular power. There are clear parallels here with the opening scene where the leaders had delivered Jesus to Pilate with the demand he be condemned under Roman law (18:28-32) and with the first public presentation of Jesus after the

[17] See the discussion in R. Brown, *The Gospel According to John XIII-XXI*, 79-80.

scourging (see 19:4-7). Now the leaders' demand is met and Jesus is delivered back to them and, ultimately, to death. Above all, this episode brings the trial, with its contest between Pilate and the leaders, to its emotional and dramatic climax as Pilate capitulates to their demands and Jesus, King of the Jews and Savior of the world, is condemned to death.

Torn between his fear of Jesus' mysterious identity and concern for his own political survival, Pilate leads Jesus out to the people for a final presentation: "He brought Jesus outside and sat on the judge's bench at a place called The Stone, or in Hebrew, Gabbatha" (19:13).

There is some intriguing uncertainty about the precise meaning of the verb "sat" *(kathizō)* in John's Greek text. It may be used in an intransitive sense—"to sit down"—as the *Revised Standard Version* translates it here. Or it can also take an object as a transitive verb and mean "to cause to sit" or "to sit (someone) down." If the evangelist was using the verb in this latter, transitive sense then it would mean that Pilate "sat (Jesus) on the judges' bench." The object ("Jesus" or "him") is not expressed but it could be that the evangelist intended to use the preceding reference to Jesus ("Pilate . . . led *Jesus* out) to serve as the object of both the verb "lead" and the verb "sit."[18] If this were the case, then we would have another striking example of Johannine irony. In a gesture of mockery or calculated insult to the Jewish leaders, Pilate unwittingly proclaims that Jesus is the authentic Judge.

But support for such a picture, no matter how appealing, is thin.[19] The verb is intransitive in the only other sure Johannine use of the verb (12:14). John's portrayal of such an extraordinary twist in the normal staging of a Roman Trial would need more elaboration than the subtlety of the verb's form. In other instances of Johannine irony, such as Pilate's question about truth

---

[18] See, especially, I. de la Potterie, "Jesus King and Judge According to John 19:13," *Scripture* 13 (1961), 97–111 and *The Hour of Jesus,* 83; W. Meeks, *The Prophet-King: Moses Traditions and the Johannine Christology* (NT Supp. 14; Leiden: Brill, 1967), 73–76. Most authors, however, are skeptical: see, for example, R. Robert, "Pilate a-t-il fait de Jésus un juge? *ekathisen epi bēmatos* (Jn 19:13)," *Revue Thomiste* 83 (1983) 275–87.

[19] The later Gospel of Peter has the Jews, not Pilate, sit Jesus upon the Judgment seat; Justin, too, refers to this scene.

(18:38) or the mock homage to Jesus as King (19-1-3), the basis for a double level of meaning is clearly set.

Uncertainty exists also concerning the place names John supplies for the location of the "judges' bench" or *bēma* (19:13). A *bēma* was a raised platform from which a presiding official would conduct business such as a trial. John notes that it is called in Greek *lithostrotos*, "stone pavement" and in Hebrew or Aramaic, *gabbatha*, which probably means a raised place or platform. The significance of this information is not immediately apparent. It may simply be that the evangelist or his sources had access to this information. Some modern interpreters believed that the "stone pavement" confirmed the location of the trial at the Antonium fortress since excavations there revealed the presence of large paving stones. However, more recently a number of archaeologists believe that these stones date to the Emperor Hadrian's rebuilding of Jerusalem at the beginning of the second century A.D. and not to the time of Herodian Jerusalem contemporary with Jesus. The term *gabbatha* could refer to the elevated place on which the *bēma* or judgment seat was placed or to the height upon which the residence of the Prefect stood.[20]

More significant for John's theological perspective is the reference to the precise time when Pilate takes his seat on the judgment bench: "Now it was the day of Preparation for the Passover; and it was about noon" (19:14). As noted above, John's chronology allows him to make full use of Passover symbolism.[21] The "sixth hour" (the term used in the Greek) would be noon, the day before the Passover. At the time of Jesus, this was the hour when the priests in the Temple would begin the slaughter of the lambs to be used in the Passover meal later that evening. Exodus 12:6 required that the lambs had to be killed "in the evening" of the preparation day. In the first century, the large number of pilgrims meant that tens of thousands of lambs needed to be slaughtered; rabbinic law, therefore, interpreted "evening" to begin at noon so that the necessary work could be completed be-

---

[20] Both traditional places, the Antonium which was built on a rock outcropping near the Temple, or Herod's palace which is in the upper part of Jerusalem, could match this description.

[21] See above, p. 77.

fore the Passover feast began at sundown.[22] Thus the judgment
condemning to death Jesus the "Lamb of God" falls precisely
at the moment the Passover lambs were being slaughtered in the
Temple.

Pilate presents Jesus to the crowd for the last time: "Here is
your King!" (19:14). In the first presentation he had appealed
to their pity in bringing the scourged and battered Jesus outside
and asking them to relent by declaring, "Here is the man!" (19:5),
a human being without power or claim to respect. Now the mood
of the drama seems different. Pilate presents Jesus as their
"king," knowing that they will not offer Jesus homage but only
rejection and death. Defeated by their unyielding determination
and their threat to his own political security, Pilate appears to
mock the Jewish leaders even as he submits to their demands. As
their cries for Jesus' crucifixion intensify, Pilate twice proclaims
Jesus as their king (19:14-15).

The drama reaches its summit with a final awful exchange:
"Shall I crucify your king? The chief priests answered, "We have
no king but the emperor" (19:15). Only a narrative steeped in
Jewish theology and Jewish symbolism could measure the terrible
irony of such a statement. In rejecting Jesus the priests have gone
too far, stripping themselves of their ancestral loyalty to God alone
as king and accepting the sovereignty of a power to which Judaism could never submit. This is hardly a historical report of what
the leaders might actually have said to Pilate. It is a strong dose
of Johannine theology. In the perspective of the Fourth Gospel,
such is the consequence of rejecting the Truth and embracing falsehood. One's very self is destroyed in a covenant with darkness.

Irony is again rampant as the forces of life and death converge.
Pilate, the Roman prefect and representative of the kings of the
earth, unwittingly proclaims the truth: Jesus is the king of the
Jews. The chief priests, representatives of Israel bound to God
in covenant and pledged to serve God alone, reject Jesus and claim
Caesar as their only king. The same priests who had feared that
the power of Rome would come and destroy Israel now give homage to that same deadly power (see 11:48).

<hr />

[22] See R. Brown, *The Gospel According to John XIII-XXI*, 882-83.

"Then he handed him over to them to be crucified" (19:16). The trial ends, punctuated by an outcome long ago predicted by Jesus and apparent to the reader from the first episode: John's wording is graphic and continues to stress the initiative of the leaders in the death of Jesus. Literally, Pilate hands Jesus over to "them," the Jewish leaders who have demanded Jesus' death. The very leaders who pledged their fealty to Caesar now do Caesar's work.

IV. Crucifixion and Death (19:17-37)

Jesus' "hour" had come. Now the Son of Man would be "lifted up" on the cross—the paradoxical throne from which this mysterious king would triumph over the world and complete the mission of salvation entrusted to him by God.

In these climactic scenes of the Passion story John continues the major themes and characteristic tones that have dominated the narrative from the moment of the arrest: by means of paradox and irony Jesus is proclaimed the true King of the world and the power of life flows from Jesus to those who believe in him; meanwhile, his foes continue their tenacious embrace of evil.

The relationship of John's account to that of the Synoptic Gospels is more tenuous here than in any other part of the Passion narrative. Key elements of the Synoptic accounts are missing in John: Simon's bearing of the cross for Jesus; the presence of the "thieves" crucified with Jesus; the mockery of the bystanders; the tearing of the temple veil; Jesus' cry of dereliction at the moment of death; and the acclamation of the centurion.

Some features of the text are, however, similar: the march from the praetorium to Golgotha (see especially Luke 23:26-32); the fact that Jesus is crucified togther with others (Luke 23:33); the casting of lots for his garments; the placement of a placard over the cross; the offer of vinegar to Jesus to drink, and the presence of women at the crucifixion site.

But John utilizes each of these elements in a manner quite different from the Synoptics and adds a number of highly charged symbolic events unique to his account: the exchange between Pilate and the Jewish leaders about the wording of the inscription (19:19-22); the seamless garment of Jesus (19:23-25a); the assignment of the mother of Jesus to the Beloved Disciple (19:25b-27); the thirst of Jesus (19:28); the manner of his death (19:30); the breaking of the legs of the other two crucified with Jesus (19:31-33); the spear thrust and the flow of blood and water from Jesus' side (19:34).

The combination of all these factors gives a unique tone to John's account. On one level John's description of the death of Jesus is more "physical" than the Synoptic versions. The divison of the condemned man's garments is described in detail; Jesus cries out in agonizing thirst; the legs of the men with him are broken to induce death; and a soldier drives a spear into Jesus' side causing blood and water to spurt from the open wound in his chest. None of the other Gospels mention any flow of blood in their entire Passion account.[1]

But arching through this surprisingly vivid description of the physical sufferings of Jesus is the commanding theological perspective of John. Jesus goes to his death with majesty, and the brutal rituals of crucifixion are transformed into symbols of triumph. Nowhere else in the Passion story is the stamp of Johannine theology more evident. Yet the profusion of symbols in this part of the narrative also makes conclusive interpretation of John's meaning a challenge.

Despite the efforts of commentators, it is difficult to assign a neatly symmetrical structure to this part of the narrative.[2] The forward motion of the story, as episode by episode leads to Jesus' death, is the determining factor in the "structure" of this sec-

---

[1] In Luke's account of the prayer in the garden, the evangelist notes that Jesus' sweat became *"like* drops of blood" (22:44); see, D. Senior, *The Passion of Jesus in the Gospel of Luke*, 87.

[2] R. Brown, for example, suggests a chaiastic pattern similar to that found in the preceding trial scene, with parallels between 19:16b-8 and 19:38-42 (elevation on the cross/burial); 19:19-22 and 19:31-37 (Pilate refuses Jew's request/Pilate grants Jew's request); 19:23-24 and 19:28-30 (executioners divide Jesus' clothers/executioners offer Jesus wine); 19:25-27 (the mother of Jesus and the Beloved Disciple) would be the middle term of the chiastic pattern: see R. Brown, *The Gospel According to John XIII-XXI*, p. 911. A number of these parallels, however, are less than obvious and the scene with the Mother of Jesus and the Beloved Disciple, while important, is not the climax of the narrative.

tion. After being turned over to the leaders by Pilate, Jesus is taken to the execution site and crucified. Despite the protests of the Jewish leaders, Pilate fixes an inscription over the cross (19:17-22). Then the narrative focuses on three final events before Jesus dies: (1) The soldiers cast lots for his seamless garment (19:23-25a); (2) Jesus entrusts his mother to the Beloved Disciple (19:25-27); (3) Jesus cries out in thirst and is given vinegar on a stalk of hyssop (19:28-29). Jesus' final words and the deliberate yielding up of his spirit bring the narrative to its zenith (19:30).

[17] So they took Jesus; and carrying the cross by himself, he went out to what is called The Place of the Skull, which in Hebrew is called Golgotha. [18] There they crucified him, and with him two others, one on either side, with Jesus between them.

[19] Pilate also had an inscription written and put on the cross. It read, "Jesus of Nazareth, the King of the Jews." [20] Many of the Jews read this inscription, because the place where Jesus was crucified was near the city; and it was written in Hebrew, in Latin, and in Greek. [21] Then the chief priests of the Jews said to Pilate, "Do not write, 'The King of the Jews,' but, 'This man said, I am King of the Jews.' " [22] Pilate answered, "What I have written I have written."

[23] When the soldiers had crucified Jesus, they took his clothes and divided them into four parts, one for each soldier. They also took his tunic; now the tunic was seamless, woven in one piece from the top. [24] so they said to one another, "Let us not tear it, but cast lots for it to see who will get it." This was to fulfill what the scripture says, "They divided my clothes among themselves, and for my clothing they cast lots." [25a] And this is what the soldiers did.

[25b] Meanwhile, standing near the cross of Jesus were his mother, and his mother's sister, Mary the wife of Clopas, and Mary Magdalene. [26] When Jesus saw his mother, and the disciple whom he loved standing beside her, he said to his mother, "Woman, here is your son." [27] Then he said to the disciple, "Here is your mother!" And from that hour the disciple took her into his own home.

[28] After this, when Jesus knew that all was now finished, he said (in order to fulfil the scripture), "I am thirsty." [29] A jar full of sour wine was standing there. So they put a sponge full of the wine on a branch of hyssop and held it to his mouth. [30] When Jesus had received the wine, he said, "It is finished." Then he bowed his head and gave up his spirit.

[31] Since it was the day of Preparation, the Jews did not want the bodies left on the cross during the sabbath because that sabbath was a day of great solemnity. So they asked Pilate to have the legs of the crucified men broken and the bodies removed. [32] Then the soldiers came and broke the legs of the first and of the other who had been crucified with him; [33] but when they came to Jesus and saw that he was already dead, they did not break his legs. [34] Instead, one of the soldiers pierced his side with a spear, and at once blood and water came out . [35] (He who saw this has testified so that you also may believe. His testimony is true, and he knows that he tells the truth.) [36] These things occurred so that the scripture might be fulfilled, "None of his bones shall be broken." [37] And again another passage of scripture says, "They will look on the one whom they have pierced."

a) *The Way to Golgotha and the Placement of the Inscription over the Cross of Jesus (19:17-22)*

This first episode in the crucifixion account keeps close continuity with the trial. Pilate had capitulated to the demands of the leaders and condemned to death the man he considered innocent and whose mysterious demeanor had unsettled him. The trial closes with the chilling words: "Then he handed him (Jesus) over to them to be crucified" (19:16). The "them" must refer to the leaders who had demanded Jesus' crucifixion (19:14b-15). The crucifixion narrative opens with the same "them" taking Jesus from Pilate, and leading him outside to the crucifixion site (19:17).

It is highly improbable that Jewish leaders actually would have carried out what was a Roman public execution and, in fact, the next verses have the soldiers in charge (19:23). But the evangelist's intent is dramatic not historically descriptive. Throughout the Gospel he has portrayed the leaders as the driving agents for Jesus' death.[3] Their blind opposition to Jesus now bears its terrible fruit as they lead Jesus to his execution site.

But another powerful Johannine current is also present here. The leaders may seem to be the instruments of Jesus' death but the reader knows that Jesus himself freely lays down his life (see 10:18). So John notes that Jesus "carrying the cross by himself, [he] went out to what is called Golgotha" (19:17). There is no Simon Cyrene to carry the cross of the Johannine Jesus (see Mark 15:21 and parallels). Some commentators note that those condemned to crucifixion may have routinely carried the crossbar or "patibulum" to the execution site, where it was fixed to a permanent upright.[4] But John's description also reflects a consistent pattern in the Passion story: Jesus is the one who takes initiative and is firmly in command of his destiny even in moments of complete vulnerability.[5]

Does the evangelist wish to evoke other layers of symbolic meaning here? Some interpreters refer to the Genesis story of the sacrifice of Isaac where the young victim carries the wood for his own sacrifice (Gen 22:6).[6] The story of Isaac's sacrifice was very important in subsequent Jewish theology but it is impossible to determine if John means to recall it here. Or does the evangelist wish to cast Jesus as a model for discipleship in the mode of the saying in Luke: "Whoever does not carry the cross and follow me, cannot be my disciple" (Lk 14:27)? John's Gospel does not report this saying of Jesus, although the notion of "following after" Jesus does occur: "Whoever serves me must follow me, and where I am, there will my servant be also" (Jn 12:26). As

---

[3] See above, Part I, pp. 39–40.

[4] See R. Brown, *The Gospel According to John XIII-XXI*, 912; for general background on the process and meaning of crucifixion in the ancient Greco-Roman world, see M. Hengel, *Crucifixion* (Philadelphia: Fortress, 1977) and J. Fitzmyer, "Crucifixion in Ancient Palestine, Qumran Literature, and the New Testament," in *To Advance the Gospel* (New York: Crossroad, 1981), 125-146.

[5] For example, Jesus confronts his captors (18:4), wins his disciples' freedom (18:8) and questions his interrogators (18:20-21, 23; 19:11); see, among others, R. Schnackenburg, *The Gospel According to St. John*, vol. 3, 270; C. K. Barrett, *The Gospel According to St. John*, 549; R. Brown, *The Gospel According to John XIII-XXI*, 917.

[6] See C. K. Barrett, *The Gospel According to St. John*, 548; R. Brown, *The Gospel According to John XIII-XXI*, 917.

is so often the case in Johannine interpretation, such secondary meanings are enticing but uncertain possibilities.

The crucifixion site is at a location "called the Place of a Skull" (19:17). John offers the Hebrew or Aramaic translation: "Golgotha." It is "outside" the city which, in fact, was the usual site for public executions, especially important in a Jewish setting so that the sacred city would not be profaned by the presence of a dead body.[7]

Whether the name "skull place" is meant to be figurative or is simply a bit of information found in the tradition available to the evangelist is unclear.[8]

The actual moment of crucifixion is described tersely, as is the case in all four Gospel accounts: "There they crucified him" (19:18a). The evangelist mentions that "two others" were also crucified with him "one on either side, with Jesus between them." The "two others" are not identified either as "bandits," as they are in Mark and Matthew (see Mk 15:27; Mt 27:38), or "evildoers" as in Luke (23:39-43). In John's version they become part of the crucified King's "retinue" as he takes his place on the throne of the cross.

The fixing of the placard over the cross reveals John's intent. As in the Synoptics it lists the crime for which Jesus is crucified: "Jesus of Nazareth, the King of the Jews" (19:19).[9] But the evangelist underscores the significance of this moment by recalling the contest between Pilate and the Jewish leaders that took place during the trial. Pilate himself composes the inscription despite the

[7] Note that Mt. 21:29 also reflects this perspective when in the allegory of the vineyard, the son is led outside of the vineyard to be killed.

[8] Some speculate that "skull" may be referring to the rock formation on which the executions took place. The traditional site of the crucifixion and burial, now located beneath the Church of the Holy Sepulchre, was in a quarry with a jumble of natural limestone caves and excisions in the rock. Or the name could have derived from the gruesome activity at this execution site. In any case, the evangelist does not seem to infer any symbolic meaning for this name in his narrative.

[9] There are minor variations among the four Gospels: Mark's stark, "The King of the Jews" (15:26, which becomes "This is the King of the Jews in Luke 22:23:48) is rendered somewhat more formally by Matthew, "This is Jesus the King of the Jews" (27:37). John's wording is the most complete, reflecting the importance of this incident for his theology. On the role of the "titulus" in the ritual of crucifixion, see E. Bammel, "The *Titulus*" in E. Bammel and C. F. D. Moule (eds.), *Jesus and the Politics of His Day* (Cambridge: Cambridge University Press, 1984), 353-64.

protests of the Jewish leaders. Pilate wanted to proclaim Jesus' identity as the "King of the Jews" to the many Jews who passed by the public execution site (19:20) so he has it written in three languages—Hebrew, Latin, and Greek.[10] The Jewish leaders vehemently oppose this, just as they had rejected Pilate's presentation of Jesus as their king in the trial (see 18:39-40; 19:14-16). They demand that Pilate change the inscription: "Do not write, "The King of the Jews,' but, "This man said, I am King of the Jews'" (19:21). But now that the outcome of the trial was determined, Pilate reserves for himself a moment of satisfaction at the leaders' expense: " 'What I have written I have written' " (19:22).

The evangelist deftly uses his ironic skill to fix all of his main characters in place. The leaders continue their self-condemning stance. They reject Jesus as their King even at the moment of his crucifixion, thereby reinforcing the terrible apostasy in their acclaim of Caesar as their king at the conclusion of the trial (see 19:15). Pilate continues in his ambivalent role: attempting to thwart the Jewish leaders in their determination to destroy Jesus, yet finally acquiesing to the crucifixion; stopping short of believing in Jesus yet strangely mystified by his true identity.

There remains another level of truth evident in this scene, the most important one that escapes both Pilate and the Jewish leaders but is clear to the reader.[11] At the moment of his crucifixion Jesus is proclaimed as King to the entire world. This is the ultimate reason he is "lifted up" on the cross; Jesus had proclaimed it so in the Gospel. "Now is the judgment of this world; now the ruler of this world be driven out. And I, when I am lifted up from the earth, will draw all people to myself" (12:31-32). The narrator had explicitly linked this to manner of Jesus' death: "He said this to indicate the kind of death he was to die" (12:33).

Thus each of the deadly details of the execution ritual are transformed and receive a new meaning: the crucifixion is the ascent of a throne; those crucified with Jesus are his retinue; the plac-

---

[10] Each of these languages would have been active in first century Palestine, with Greek, and to a lesser extent, Latin, the languages of commerce. Aramaic would be the native tongue of the Jewish population, with Hebrew more of a "liturgical" or religious language.

[11] P. Duke sees this as another supreme instance of Johannine irony: see, *Irony in the Fourth Gospel,* 136-37; also R. A. Culpepper, *Anatomy of the Fourth Gospel,* 174.

ing of the inscription becomes the proclamation of Jesus' royal status; the multiple languages of the inscription and the public site of the execution insure the universal transmission of Jesus' message; Pilate's insistence becomes the means whereby Jesus' identity is revealed despite the hostility of the Jewish leaders and the Roman prefect's own corruption.

The sense of triumph—so transparent in John's Gospel—shimmers through the darkest moment of Jesus' life.

b) *The Soldiers Cast Lots for Jesus' Seamless Garment (19:23-25a)*

In each of the Gospels the Roman soldiers cast lots to decide who will receive the garments of the man they have executed. John dwells on this incident in a way that suggests to many interpreters he intends some deeper significance for this incident.

The soldiers divide Jesus' clothing into four parts, one for each of them. The Greek word used here for "clothes" *(himatia)* usually means the outer garment. But they decide not to divide the "tunic" *(chiton)*—the inner or undergarment—because it was "without seam, woven from top to bottom" (19:23). For this seamless garment they cast lots "to see whose it shall be" (19:24). In so doing, the evangelist notes, the soldiers unwittingly fulfilled the Scripture, "They divided my garments among themselves, and for my clothing they cast lots" (19:24).

The quotation is from Psalm 22:19 which describes the torments of the Just One of Israel, surrounded by enemies and crying out to God for deliverance. This eloquent lament Psalm was an important point of reference for all of the Passion narratives, particularly those of Matthew and Mark.[1] The Johannine account insures the literal fufillment of the words of the Psalm. The original lament has the typical parallelism of Hebrew poetry: the "parting" of the garments and the "casting of lots" are one and the same action described in two parallel ways. But John takes each part of the parallel and applies it to two separate actions of the

---

[1] The great lament Psalm 22 plays an important role in the Passion tradition, particularly in the Gospel of Mark and Matthew, where the first verse of the Psalm is on Jesus' lips as he dies (Mk 15:34; Mt 27:46, 50; see the discussion of these verses in D. Senior, *The Passion of Jesus in the Gospel of Mark*, 118, 123-24; *The Passion of Jesus in the Gospel of Matthew*, 136-41).

soldiers: the dividing of Jesus' outer garments and the casting of lots for the inner, seamless garment.

For some interpreters this is a sign that the evangelist misunderstood the original parallelism of the Psalm.[2] However, Matthew's Gospel makes the same kind of literal application of a quotation from Zechariah 9:9 in describing the "ass and the colt" on which Jesus enters Jerusalem (see Mt. 21:4-7), suggesting a conscious use of the artifice in Jewish interpretation. The reference to the Psalm was probably already present in the tradition prior to John and the evangelist reinforces it. In any case John wishes to affirm that the events of the crucifixion fulfilled the Hebrew Scriptures, demonstrating once again that Jesus' death is not a historical accident but part of God's plan of salvation.

But is there another level of symbolism present? Harmony with the quotation from Psalm 22 could have been achieved without the insistence on the seamless quality of Jesus' garments. Many interpreters find further symbolic meaning in this detail. The description of the tunic as "seamless" and "woven in one piece from the top" may be intended to recall the vestments of the High Priest.[3] The vestments are described in some detail in Exodus 28 (see also Ex 39:27-31; Leviticus 16:4) but there is no mention of their being "seamless." The Jewish historian Josephus, however, does refer to this quality: "Now this vesture (of the High Priest) was not composed of two pieces, nor was it sewed together upon the shoulders and the sides, but it was one long vestment so woven as to have an aperture for the neck; not an oblique one, but parted all along the breast and the back."[4]

Did the evangelist, therefore, want to suggest that Jesus was the "high priest" about to sacrifice himself on behalf of the world? John's Gospel does exploit Passover symbolism in connection with the death of Jesus, but there is little evidence that the evangelist interpreted Jesus himself as Priest in connection

---

[2] See C. K. Barrett, *The Gospel According to St. John*, 549.

[3] See the discussion in I. de la Potterie, "La tunique sans couture, symbôle du Christ grand prêtre?" *Biblica* 60 (1979) 255–69, and in *The Hour of Jesus*, 98–104 who doubts that a reference to the High Priest's vestments is possible and prefers a symbol of unity instead.

[4] F. Josephus, *The Antiquities of the Jews*, (trans. W. Whiston; Peabody, MA: Hendrickson, 1987); Book 3, chapter 7, #161.

with his death.[5] The Letter to the Hebrews portrays Jesus as the High Priest of the new cult but does not play upon the symbol of the vestments and, in any case, would not be support for interpreting the meaning of John 19:23.

Other commentators prefer to see an emphasis on unity in this Johannine incident.[6] The seamless nature of Jesus' garment and the soldiers' decision not to divide it would be symbolic of the unity Jesus creates through his mission to the world. Certainly "unity" is a Johannine concern, one reinforced in chapter 17, immediately prior to the Passion.

> "I ask not only on behalf of these, but also on behalf of those who believe in me through their word, that they may all be one. As you, Father, are in me, and I am in you, may they also may be in us, so that the world may believe that you have sent me." (17:20-21).

Both of these suggestions are tantalizing but impossible to prove. The fact that this incident fulfills the Scriptures—thereby reinforcing the God-endorsed destiny of Jesus—is clearly John's intent, but additional symbolic meanings are uncertain.[7]

However, this incident has another function in the flow of John's Passion narrative. On the literal level of the text, the action of the soldiers, whatever symbolic or theological meanings may be present, is hostile in intent. They divide up and confiscate the worldly possessions of the innocent man they are executing. That cold and brutal ritual of the Roman soldiers sets up a sharp contrast with the next scene where the reader learns of the faithful presence of the women and the Beloved Disciple at the cross and sees the way Jesus himself will care for what belongs to him (19:25b-27).

[5] The Johannine Jesus does speak of "consecrating himself" for the sake of the disciples (17:19), which is cultic language, but it is not apparent that John interprets the death of Jesus in this manner.

[6] See, for example, the references to de la Potterie, above; also C. K. Barrett, *The Gospel According to St. John,* 550.

[7] See the caution expressed in B. Lindars, *The Gospel of John,* 578; G. Beasley-Murray, *John,* 347-48, among others. R. Schnackenburg suggests that Jesus is, in effect, putting aside his garments in preparation for death as he did at the supper (13:4); God continues to protect Jesus even at this moment of destitution in that the garment is not destroyed: see *The Gospel According to John,* vol. 3, 273-74. But this interpretation seems no more compelling than the traditional explanations.

c) *The Mother of Jesus and the Beloved Disciple (19:25b-27)*

This episode is one of the most appealing yet enigmatic scenes of John's Passion narrative. As the moment of death approaches, Jesus turns to his mother and entrusts her to the care of his Beloved Disciple. On one level, it is a touching and gracious gesture of a faithful son as he nears death. But does the evangelist intend something more? Based on the importance the evangelist seems to assign this incident and its connection with previous events in the Gospel, many commentators detect here a deep theological significance.

The only connection with the Synoptic tradition is the mention of women at the crucifixion site (19:25).[1] However, even in this John's Gospel diverges from the others. Each of the Synoptics mention the women's presence *after* the death of Jesus and note that they stood "at a distance" (Lk 23:49; Mk 15:40 and Mt 27:55 mention they were looking on "from afar"); in John they are standing *"near* the cross of Jesus" (19:25) and are noted as present *before* he dies. Mary Magdalene is the only one listed in all four Gospels and none of the others mention the presence of the mother of Jesus or of the Beloved Disciple.[2] Only John has Jesus interact with the people who are present.

There is little doubt that the evangelist gives this scene considerable significance. The entrusting of his mother to the Beloved Disciple signals the completion of Jesus' work: "After this, (i.e., his words to his mother and the disciple) when Jesus knew that all was now finished . . ." (19:28)[3] Why is this scene so important that it becomes the final act of Jesus's life?

Interpretations vary tremendously. Some conclude that the scene has no special theological significance at all. Jesus as a good

---

[1] Mark 15:40-41 mentions Mary Magdalene, Mary the mother of James the younger and of Joses, and Salome; Mt 27:56 refers to Mary Magdalene, Mary the mother of James *and Joseph,* and "the mother of the Sons of Zebedee"; Lk 23:49 simply notes "the women who had followed him from Galilee" without citing any names. John lists "his mother, his mother's sister, Mary, the wife of Clopas, and Mary Magdalene" (19:25); it is not certain whether "Mary, the wife of Clopas" is "his mother's sister" or a distinct individual; see the discussion in R. Brown, *The Gospel According to John XIII-XXI,* 904–06.

[2] Luke may be alluding to the presence of Jesus' disciples when he mentions that "all those who knew (Jesus)" were there (Lk 23:49).

[3] See below, pp. 114–15.

and compassionate man took care of his mother by entrusting her to his beloved disciple, thus ensuring her care after his death. A widow was vulnerable and so Jesus acts both justly and with care. As mentioned earlier, the scene also serves as a vivid constrast with the previous episode where the soldiers cast lots for Jesus' garments. The faithful women and the Beloved Disciple are a counterpart to the hostile presence of the soldiers, and Jesus' gracious act of entrusting his mother to the disciple contrasts with the rapacious character of the executioners.

But many others believe this does not take into account all the dimensions of the text. First of all, Jesus does not address Mary as "mother" but as "woman"—reminiscent of the same address used of her in the Cana story (2:4). If the care of a son for his mother was the sole meaning of the scene at the cross, one might expect the address "mother" to be used. This designation for the mother of Jesus and the reference to the "hour" in the Cana story suggest that the evangelist intends to link these two stories.

Secondly, the presence of the Beloved Disciple—without Peter for the first time in John's Gospel—also may signal that this scene has particular importance for the evangelist. The presence of a disciple with the mother of Jesus is another link to the Cana scene where Jesus' disciples, together with his mother, also play a role (2:2,11). Finally, the climactic placement of this episode immediately prior to the death scene also argues in favor of some deeper symbolic meaning.

But there is no clear consensus on what this deeper theological meaning might be. Some Roman Catholic authors have used this text to illustrate traditional affirmations of Mariology.[4] For example, Mary is hereby proclaimed as sharing in Jesus' redemptive act by being associated with him at the hour of his death, becoming a kind of "co-redemptrix" with Jesus. Or Mary is proclaimed as the "New Eve," fulfilling the promise of the

---

[4] See the discussion in J. McHugh who reviews the works of F. -M. Braun and A. Feuillet on this score: *The Mother of Jesus in the New Testament* (Garden City: Doubleday, 1975), 361–403; and R. Brown, *The Gospel According to John XIII-XXI*, 922-27; R. Brown et alii, *Mary in the New Testament* (New York: Paulist, 1978), 206–18; J. Grassi, "The Role of Jesus' Mother in John's Gospel," *Catholic Biblical Quarterly* 48 (1986), 67–80; P. Perkins, "Mary in Johannine Traditions," in D. Donnelly (ed.), *Mary, Woman of Nazareth* (New York: Paulist, 1989), 109–22.

"woman" in Genesis 3:15 who will finally crush the head of evil by her association with the redemptive act of Jesus.[5] Such reflections on Mary, whatever may be their theological merit in Church tradition, find no explicit support in the Gospel and go beyond what the Johannine text affirms.

Other interpretations work more closely within the parameters of Johannine symbolism. Three major lines of interpretation can be traced:

1) This passage is not focused on the Mother of Jesus but on the *Beloved Disciple.* In this interpretation, the evangelist's point is to validate the testimony of the Beloved Disciple by portraying him as a member of the "family" of Jesus on the basis of Jesus' own declaration. In the Synoptic tradition, Jesus declares that his disciples are indeed members of his household: " 'Who are my mother and my brothers?' And looking at those who sat around him, he said, 'Here are my mother and my brothers! Whoever does the will of God is my brother and sister and mother.' " (Mk 3:31-35 and parallels). The scene at the cross focuses that "adoption" on the Beloved Disciple, one who had paramount importance for the Johannine community and whose testimony about the death of Jesus is a cornerstone of the Johannine tradition (see 19:35).

The weakness of this interpretation is that it focuses on only one dimension of the scene—the Beloved Disciple—and does not take up the possible symbolic meaning of the "woman."

2) Others find an *ecclesial significance* in the scene. The mother of Jesus is symbolic of Lady Sion or Judaism and thus represents the Jewish Christian community, while the Beloved Disciple represents the new Gentile community. The Jewish Christians are thus to find a "home" in the emerging Gentile Church.

While such a reading of the scene is enticing, there is no clear evidence in the Fourth Gospel that John portrays the mother of Jesus in this way, nor that the Beloved Disciple represents the Gentile Christians.

3) Still others find *salvific* meaning implied in this scene. There

---

[5] This interpretation draws also on Revelation 12; see the discussion of the evidence in R. Brown, *Mary in the New Testament,* 219-39.

are several variations here and each of them relate the scene at the cross with earlier strands of John's Gospel.

Raymond Brown, for example, takes his cues both from the Cana scene and from the image of the woman giving birth in Jn 16:21. The Cana story portrays the mother of Jesus making a claim upon him prior to the "hour" when his mission would be completed, but Jesus turns the attention of the reader to the Passion and his death (2:4). Thus the messianic abundance previewed in the changing of water to wine will find its realization at the death of Jesus. The presence at the cross of the mother of Jesus and the premier disciple of the Johannine community illustrate the abundant new life that flows into the world through the death of Jesus.

The image of the woman in labor in 16:21 adds another strand to the text:

> "When a woman is in labor, she has pain, because her hour has come. But when her child is born, she no longer remembers the anguish because of the joy of having brought a human being into the world."

This Johannine image, in turn, evokes passages in Isaiah which portray exiled Israel in torment and labor, yearning to bring forth new life from its barrenness:

> "The children born in the time of your bereavement will yet say in your hearing; 'The place is too crowded for me; make room for me to settle.' Then you will say in your heart: 'Who has borne me these? I was bereaved and barren, exiled and put away—so who has reared these? I was left alone—where then have these come from?' " (Isaiah 49:20-22)

> "Sing, O Barren one who did not bear; burst into song and shout, you who have not been in labor! For the children of the desolate woman will be more than the children of her that is married, says the Lord." (Isaiah 54:1)

> "Before she was in labor she gave birth; before her pain came upon her she delivered a son. Who has heard such a thing? Who has seen such things? Shall a land be born in one day? Shall

a nation be delivered in one moment? Yet as soon as Zion was in labor she delivered her children. Shall I open the womb and not deliver? says the Lord; shall I, the one who delivers, shut the womb? says your God." (Isaiah 66:7-11)

Does, then, John wish to evoke this tradition of Sion giving birth to new life through God's powerful intervention? Despite the travail of the death of Jesus and paradoxically even *through* that travail, the mother of Jesus—the "woman" Sion—brings forth new life in the form of the Beloved Disciple and the community he represents. This "completes" the work of Jesus, bringing his act of love to its goal in creating the church, as he had stated in the opening lines of the Book of Glory. Jesus had loved his own and would love them "to the end" (see 13:1). For this reason, once Jesus has entrusted his mother to the Beloved Disciple, the evangelist can make the decisive transition expressed in 19:28: "After this when Jesus, *knew that all was now finished* . . ."

Rudolf Schnackenburg has proposed an interpretation similar but not identical to that of Brown.[6] The mother of Jesus is symbolic of those who seek salvation, a quest fulfilled at the cross of Jesus. The link to the Cana story is key. There the Mother of Jesus is represented as one who expects salvation from Jesus; this is the point of her approach to her son (2:3) and her confident instruction to the attendants (2:5).

In this role the Mother of Jesus may also represent those believing Jews who are longing for messianic salvation, some of whom are portrayed in the Gospel. John the Baptist, for example, states that his mission is to have the Messiah Jesus "revealed to Israel" (1:31); Andrew joyfully tells his brother Simon, "We have found the Messiah" (1:41) and Philip announces to Nathanael, "We have found him about whom Moses in the law and also the prophets wrote, Jesus son of Joseph from Nazareth" (1:45); finally, Nathanael comes to acclaim Jesus: "Rabbi, you are the Son of God! You are the King of Israel!" (1:49). The crowds similarly acclaim Jesus as he triumphantly enters Jerusalem: "Ho-

6 R. Schnackenburg, *The Gospel According To St. John*, vol. 3, 277-82.

sanna! Blessed is the one who comes in the name of the Lord, the King of Israel!" (12:13).

The mother of Jesus, therefore, is representative of that part of Israel which longed for salvation and found it in Jesus. She is entrusted to the Beloved Disciple, representative of the Johannine community, the locus where vital contact with the salvation wrought through Jesus continues to be found. This is the role that the Beloved Disciple plays in the Gospel. He is close to Jesus and the recipient of private instruction (13:23-26); he believes in Jesus (20:8), understands his teaching and gives witness to it (19:35: 21:7).

Therefore, the faithful Jews who discover salvation in Jesus are entrusted to the church; the "mother" is entrusted to the son (19:26). But, at the same time, the Beloved Disciple is asked to recognize the woman as his mother (19:27). The Christian community is reminded of the "mother"—Judaism—from whom salvation comes (4:22) and from whom the community itself originated.[7]

It is impossible to reconcile all of these variant interpretations of John's scene because the symbolic character of the episode makes precision difficult. There are, however, some common threads worth noting:

a) The climactic nature of this scene as the "completion" of Jesus' life means that John intends more than a surface reading of the episode; i.e., it is more than the gracious act of a dutiful son and more than a contrast with the actions of the soldiers in the previous scene.

b) The link to the Cana story—where the mother of Jesus, his disciples, and reference to the "hour" of Jesus' death are all present—is important. At Cana the mother of Jesus seeks assistance from her son, but on a deeper level such assistance (= salvation?) must await the "hour" of Jesus' death.

c) The role of the Beloved Disciple as representative of the Jo-

---

[7] R. Schnackenburg, *The Gospel According to St. John,* vol. 3, 278. Note that in John's Gospel, the first disciples of Jesus are drawn from the disciples of the Baptist, the exemplar of believing and expectant Israel (1:35-51); see F. Segovia, "Discipleship in the Fourth Gospel," in F. Segovia (ed.), *Discipleship in the New Testament* (Philadelphia: Fortress, 1985), 80–82.

hannine community is also key to the meaning of the scene at the cross.

d) Although it is less certain, the tie to 16:21 may also offer a further clue to the symbolic meaning of the mother of Jesus in the episode at the cross; she is the "woman" in travail bringing forth a new "son."

Binding these threads together makes the "salvific" interpretation of the episode persuasive. The mother of Jesus—the "woman"—is symbolic of those who seek salvation and of that people who have longed for and will in fact give birth to the messiah, Jesus. That "birthing" takes place at the cross when Jesus completes his work and returns to the Father. The first impact of Jesus' death—anticipated in 19:26-27—is the birth of the Johannine community. The Beloved Disciple represents that community who believes in Jesus and continues his revelation to the world. Those Israelites open to the truth and searching for the Messiah are entrusted to this community of faith and, in turn, the church is to recognize its roots in the faith of Israel.

Giving birth to the Church is, in John's theology, the first consequence and the first sign of Jesus' redemptive death. The entrusting of the mother of Jesus to the Beloved Disciple is an exquisite symbol of that; so, too, will be the blood and water that spring from the open side of the Crucified Jesus (see 19:34-37).

d) *The Death of Jesus (19:28-30)*

Jesus meets death with the same deliberation and majestic calm that has characterized his entire Passion in John's Gospel. Not unexpectedly, John's version of the death scene is distinctive in comparison to the Synoptic accounts. There is no cry of dereliction and no final mockery. Jesus is in full control even as his life ends. And in the usual Johannine fashion the scene is filled with rich and sometimes enigmatic symbolism.

The entrusting of his mother to the Beloved Disciple is the final work Jesus performs; his mission of salvation is assured as believing Israel is merged with the community of the Beloved Disciple (see above, 19:25-27). The Church will be born at the moment of Jesus' death. "After this" Jesus knows "that all was now finished" (19:28). The emphasis on Jesus' prophetic knowledge is also typical of John's powerful christology.[1]

The Greek verb used for "complete" or "finish" is *teleō*, a word with particular significance in John. Several times this verb or its derivitive is used in summary statements of Jesus' mission, a mission described as "completing the work(s)" entrusted to Jesus by the Father. When the disciples had pressed him to eat during his visit to Samaria, Jesus had replied "I have food to eat of which you do not know." They thought someone had brought him food, but he pressed beyond their misunderstanding: "My food is to do the will of him who sent me and to complete *(teleiōsō)* his work" (4:34). Similarly, in a dispute with the Jewish leaders, Jesus stated: ". . . the works that the Father has given me to complete *(teleiōsō)*, the very works that I am doing, testify on my behalf that the Father has sent me" (5:36). At the beginning of the "High Priestly Prayer" in chapter 17 the same phrase is asserted again: "I glorified you on earth by finishing *(teleiōsas)* the work that you gave me to do" (17:4).

Now at the moment of death that great "work" of Jesus was about to be "completed." This transition verse has strong parallels with 13:1, the opening verse of the Book of Glory: "Now before the festival of the Passover, Jesus knew that his hour had come to depart from this world and go to the Father. Having loved his own who were in the world, he loved them to the end *(telos)*." The evangelist describes Jesus' death with two characteristic Johannine terms: Jesus is about to "depart from this world to the Father" and "loving his own . . . to the end." The death of Jesus is at once a moment of exaltation in returning to his Father and a self-sacrificing act of friendship love for "his own." Mounted on his cross-throne, Jesus is about to complete this great work.

A final word is spoken: "I am thirsty" (19:28). This, too, is a unique Johannine touch. In Mark and Matthew Jesus is offered a sponge filled with vinegar after he cries out the words of Psalm 22. The bystanders mistake (or mock) his prayer *"Eli"* ("My God") as an invocation of "Elijah" (see Mk 15:35-56; Mt. 27:47-48). In Luke the offer of vinegar is clearly designated as an act of mockery on the part of the Roman soldiers (see Lk

[1] See, for example, 13:1, 21; 18:4.

23:37).[2] But in none of these instances does Jesus cry out in thirst nor does he drink the vinegar offered to him.

John's scene is completely different. Jesus is conscious that the moment of death is at hand, and therefore he deliberately cries out: "I am thirsty." This act, the evangelist emphasizes, is done "in order to fulfill the scripture" (19:28). A sponge full of vinegar is put on "hyssop" and raised to his lips (19:29). Jesus takes the vinegar and then declares: "It is finished." With this act and this word, he dies (19:30).

Obviously in the Johannine account, the thirst of Jesus has profound meaning. The Gospel ties the words "I am thirsty" to the fulfillment of Scripture. This probably refers to such texts as Psalm 69:21 which speaks of the vinegar—"They gave me poison for food, and for my thirst they gave me vinegar to drink"— and Psalm 22:16 which describes the thirst of the suffering just man—"my mouth is dried up like a potsherd, and my tongue sticks to my jaws; you lay me in the dust of death." Both psalms play a key role in the Passion tradition and the episode of giving vinegar to Jesus at the moment of his crucifixion undoubtedly is linked to the psalms in all four Gospels.[3]

But John's incident goes beyond this traditional note of scriptural fulfillment. In fact the word used is not "fulfill" but "complete" *(teleiōthei)* the Scriptures, the same verb discussed above. With his cry of thirst and the drinking of the vinegar Jesus "completes" the Scriptures. Obviously something more than a mockery or torment imposed on the dying Jesus is signified in this act. The key may be the reference to the drinking of the cup in 18:11.[4] At that moment of violence in the garden, Jesus had rebuked Peter and told him to put his sword back into its sheath. Jesus would not swerve from his God-given mission: "Am I not to *drink the cup* that the Father has given me?" (18:11).

Completing the work of the Father—giving his life out of love for the world and thus returning in exaltation to God—this was

---

[2] This compensates for the omission of mockery during the trial; see D. Senior, *The Passion of Jesus in the Gospel of Luke,* 132.

[3] Note that the evangelist has already appealed to Psalm 69 in 2:17 (see Psalm 69:9) and 15:25 (see Psalm 69:4); see further, R. Brown, *The Gospel According to John XIII-XXI,* 929.

[4] See R. Brown, *The Gospel According to John XIII-XXI,* 911; R. Schnackenburg, *The Gospel According to St. John,* vol. 3, 283–84.

"food" Jesus would eat (4:34) and the "cup" he would drink (18:11). This, in John's portrayal, was the driving force of Jesus' mission. Therefore the cry of thirst that echoes over Golgotha is no longer a cry of torment—as the onlookers wrongly suppose—but a final act of commitment. Jesus thirsts for God and he thirsts out of love for "his own in this world."

This act "completes" all of the work of God promised in the Scriptures because it is the definitive act of redemption foreshadowed in all of God's actions on behalf of Israel.[5] The epic lines of the prologue come to mind: "the law was given through Moses; grace and truth came through Jesus Christ" (1:17).[6]

The reference to "hyssop" may also be symbolic. Mark and Matthew refer to a "reed" on which the bystanders place the sponge full of vinegar (see Mk 15:36; Mt 27:48). Hyssop is ill suited for the task of holding up a vinegar soaked sponge since it is leafy and pliant. However, John may intend to evoke the Passover symbolism that has run through the Passion story.[7] In order to spare the Israelites at the the moment of Exodus Moses commanded the elders to,

> "Take a bunch of hyssop, dip it in the blood that is in the basin, and touch the lintel and the two doorposts with the blood in the basin . . . For the Lord will pass through to strike the Egyptians; when he sees the blood on the lintel and on the two doorposts, the Lord will pass over that door and will not allow the destroyer to enter your houses to strike you down." (Exodus 12:22-23).

The letter to the Hebrews recalls the sprinkling of blood with "hyssop" that sealed the covenant (9:18-20) in describing Jesus as the mediator of a new covenant forged in the blood of Christ.

Does the evangelist wish to evoke this Passover symbolism here? The Gospel has already emphasized that this was the Day of

[5] See B. Lindars, *The Gospel of John,* 580; C. K. Barrett, *The Gospel According to St. John,* 553.

[6] The verse implies a contrast with the period of "Moses"; while "fulfillment" terminology is not prevalent in John, the evangelist clearly sees Jesus as eclipsing all previous moments in salvation history.

[7] See above, pp. 33–34.

Preparation (see 19:14, 31) and the very hour in which the Pass-over lambs were being slain in the Temple in preparation for the Passover celebration. Now the Lamb of God was offering him-self for slaughter that the world might live.[8]

Johannine irony is at work again in the Passion story. On the literal level of the text, the soldiers who oversee the execution of this messianic pretender respond to his cry of thirst by thrusting a vinegar soaked sponge on a stalk of hyssop to his lips. It is a pitiful, perhaps even contemptuous gesture towards one who dies apparently without hope or resources. But the reader sees and hears something very different. Jesus' cry of thirst is a deliberate act, reaffirming in the face of death his complete freedom and unswerving commitment to the mission God had entrusted to him. He thirsts because he desires deeply to "drink" the cup given to him—the cup that will complete the work he has been given to do, the work of loving his own in the world until the end. The blood of his death will bring a deliverance foreshadowed in the liberation of Israel from slavery.

Thus this radical thirst of Jesus completes all of the sacred promises of the Scriptures and brings the mission of Jesus to its summit. One final word is spoken, a word in perfect harmony with the tone of the entire Johannine Passion story: "It is fin-ished *(tetelestai)"* (19:30). The same verb, used twice before in this scene (see 19:28), brings the life of Jesus to its goal. He has "completed" his work and returned to God.

Each Gospel writer crafts the final instant of Jesus' life in a manner consistent with the Gospel's overall portrayal. In Mark's Gospel, Jesus dies with a wordless scream, the final act of the Son of Man who had come to serve (Mk 15:37). In Matthew, Jesus cries out once again the wrenching words of lament found in Psalm 22, reaffirming in the midst of pain and dereliction, the abiding trust of the Son of God in his Father (Mt 27:50). In Luke's account, Jesus, prophet, martyr, and just man, dies confidently, entrusting his spirit to God (Lk 23:46). For John, too, the por-trait is consistent: Jesus dies with majestic assurance. The mis-sion of redemptive love that brought the Word to flesh and

---

[8] See, also C. K. Barrett, *The Gospel According to St. John,* 553; R. Brown, *The Gospel According to John XIII-XXI,* 930.

animated his signs and life-giving words now reaches its summit and completion at the instant of death.[9]

The moment of death is described in a way that fits this tone of completion. Jesus "bowed his head and gave up his spirit" (19:30). The verb "gave up" in Greek is *"paredōken."* This word was used repeatedly to describe the "handing over" of Jesus to his captors and ultimately to death itself.[10] But here it takes on a different connotation, that of a deliberate and serene "handing over" of Jesus' life spirit to God. Jesus' enemies had supposed themselves to be in control of his destiny by handing him over to a violent death. But, in fact, Jesus, in communion with his God, was the one who would enact his own deliverance to death and thereby complete his God-given mission.

The Greek term for "spirit" is *pneuma,* the identical word used for the Holy Spirit.[11] Some commentators conclude that the evangelist may be implying that Jesus diffuses the Spirit upon the world in this instant of death, in effect fulfilling the prophecy of 7:38-39. It is certainly compatible with Johannine theology to link the donation of the Spirit with the death of Jesus (see 7:39). But John will assert this symbolically in the flow of water from the side of the crucified Jesus (see below, 19:34) and in the resurrection appearance where the Risen Jesus "breathes" upon the disciples and declares: "Receive the Holy Spirit *(pneuma hagion)"* (20:22). The phrase "hand over his spirit" in 19:30 refers to the moment of death itself and the focus is on Jesus' return to God. While a double-meaning cannot be excluded for such a phrase, it is more likely that the evangelist does not intend to describe at this point the donation of the Spirit.

The overall impact of the death scene is unambiguous. Jesus meets death and triumphs over it. The bold declaration of 10:17-18 finds its fulfillment here:

> "For this reason the Father loves me, because I lay down my life in order to take it up again. No one takes it from me, but

[9] See, M. Thompson, *The Humanity of Jesus in the Fourth Gospel* (Philadelphia: Fortress, 1988), 108–109.

[10] See 18:2, 5, 30, 35, 36; 19:11, 16.

[11] See John 1:32, 33; 3:5, 6, 8, 34; 4:23, 24; 6:63; 7:39; 14:17, 26; 15:26; 16:13; 20:22.

I lay it down of my own accord. I have power to lay it down, and I have power to take it again. I have received this command from my Father."[12]

The creation of a new "family" of Jesus (19:25-27) had already signaled what this final act of love would mean for the world. Equally telling signs will make their appearance in the scenes that follow.

e) *Signs of New Life: The Flow of Blood and Water and Jesus as the Paschal Lamb Whose Bones cannot be Broken (19:31-37)*

The evangelist extends his use of irony to the very end of the Passion story. The final rites of public execution, the coup de grace, become in the Johannine account a means for proclaiming the life-giving impact of the death of Jesus. This scene is unique to John. Its only parallel with the Synoptic accounts is the fact that immediately following the death of Jesus come the prodigious signs of the tearing of the temple veil (Mark and Matthew), the opening of the graves (Matthew) and acclamations by the Centurion (Mark, Matthew, Luke)—each of them awesome results of Jesus' death.

But the events in John's account are not prodigious or awe-inspiring in themselves; in fact, on the surface they are further brutalities inflicted on Jesus. But the evangelist gives the reader clear signals that these events are signs of deeper, wondrous realities streaming from the life-giving death of Jesus.

The enemies of Jesus reinsert themselves into the drama. Because it was the "Day of Preparation" (the eve of Passover), and also the eve of Sabbath—the Passover and Sabbath fell on the same day that year in John's chronology—the Jewish leaders fear contamination if the bodies remain on the cross (19:31). Deuteronomy 21:23 had commanded that the body of one "hung on a tree" should not be allowed to remain all night on the gibbet, "you shall bury him that same day, for anyone hung on a tree is under God's curse. You must not defile the land that the Lord

[12] See R. Schnackenburg, *The Gospel According to St. John,* vol. 3, 285; Note that a different Greek verb *(tithēmi)* is used for "lay down" in 10:17-18.

your God is giving you for possession." The leaders' concern for cultic purity—even as their determination to destroy Jesus is slaked—recalls the touch of irony with which the trial scene had begun. The leaders had feared to enter the Praetorium "so as to avoid ritual defilement" (18:28).

The leaders, therefore, ask that the legs of the crucified men be broken. Hastening death by the shock of breaking the limbs of a crucified victim was apparently normal procedure.[1] As at the beginning of the trial, Pilate accedes to the wishes of the Jews without comment. The soldiers begin by breaking the legs of the two men crucified on each side of Jesus (19:32; see 19:18) but when they discover that Jesus is already dead they decide not to break his legs. For the Gospel this is not an accident but a moment of deep significance, one that "fulfills the Scripture" (see below, 19:36).

The decision not to break Jesus' bones leads, however, to another brutality to which the evangelist attaches profound meaning. One of the soldiers thrusts a lance into Jesus' chest (literally, "his side") and immediately "blood and water" flow out (19:34). The Gospel leaves no doubt that this flow of blood and water from the crucified and dead Jesus is of great significance. The narrator breaks into the description and gives testimony: "He who saw this has testified that you also may believe. His testimony is true, and he knows that he tells the truth." (19:35). And, like the decision not to break Jesus' legs, the piercing of Jesus' side and the flow of blood and water fulfill the Scriptures (19:37).

THE MEANING OF THE SIGNS

In the testimony of the eye-witness, these events are intended to ignite the faith of those to whom the Gospel is proclaimed (19:35). What precisely is the meaning of these two signs?

[1] See recent discovery of the remains of a Palestinian victim of crucifixion with his tibia broken, probably in the act of crucifixion; J. Fitzmyer, *To Advance the Gospel* (New York: Crossroad, 1981), 126–29; J. Charlesworth, *Jesus Within Judaism* (Garden City: Doubleday, 1988), 122–23.

"None of his bones shall be broken"

The fact that Jesus' legs are not broken seems to be yet another instance where the Johannine author uses Passover symbolism to interpret the death of Jesus. The Scripture text cited in 19:36—"None of his bones shall be broken"—paraphrases several biblical descriptions of the Paschal lamb. Exodus instructs that "you shall not break any of its bones" (Exodus 12:46) and further mandates that the lamb is to be consumed intact "with its head, legs and inner organs" (12:9). None of it is to "remain until the morning" (12:10). Similarly Numbers 9:12 states "They shall leave none of it until morning, nor break a bone of it; according to all the statutes for the passover they shall keep it." Coupled with the several chronological references to the Passover in John's Passion narrative, there seems little doubt that the evangelist intends here to reinforce his portrayal of Jesus as the "Lamb of God" who gives his life "to take away the sin of the world" (1:29, 35).[2]

Some commentators see another possible allusion in 19:36. Psalm 34 hymns Yahweh's protection of the righteous one, even as this just Israelite is surrounded by evildoers. The Lord "keeps all his bones; not one of them is broken" (Psalm 34:30). Does the evangelist intend to portray Jesus also as the righteous one who suffers unjustly but is protected by God?[3] The reference in Psalm 34 has the advantage of a personal referent (i.e., "his bones") which brings it into closer alignment with John 19:36. The theme of God's protection and ultimate vindication of the righteous sufferer also coincides with the note of triumph evident in the Johannine death scene. Here is another instance in which a double level of symbolism cannot be excluded.

"They will look on the one whom they have pierced"

The flow of blood and water from the lanced side of Jesus is also richly laden with meaning. Clearly the evangelist gives sym-

---

[2] See above, pp. 33–34.

[3] See, for example, R. Brown, *The Gospel According to John XIII–XXII*, 953. The theme of the suffering just man is important in the Synoptic Passion accounts; see, for example, D. Senior, *The Passion of Jesus in the Gospel of Matthew*, 134–35.

bolic meaning to the "blood and water" but, as is often the case with Johannine symbols, the precise meaning is tantalizingly imprecise.

The "water" symbol is probably the easier of the two to interpret since the Gospel itself has connected it with the gift of the Spirit brought through the death of Jesus. The link between "water" and "Spirit" begins early in the Gospel. John testifies that he baptizes "with water" (1:26, 31, 33) but only to reveal Jesus, the one who will baptize "with the Holy Spirit" (1:33). The theme is resumed in the discussion with Nicodemus. Jesus declares that "unless one is born of water and the Spirit, one cannot enter the kingdom of God" (3:5). The Samaritan woman who encounters Jesus at the well is told that he bears the gift of "living water" (4:10) and that "Everyone who drinks of this water will be thirsty again, . . . The water that I will give will become in them a spring of water gushing up to eternal life." (4:14).

A decisive text is that of 7:37-39. The Gospel places Jesus' words against the backdrop of the Jewish feast of Sukkoth or Tabernacles. During this weeklong feast Israel prayed for the onset of the Fall rains, climaxing with a procession from the pool of Siloam to the altar of the Temple. At this dramatic moment on the last day of the festival, Jesus proclaims:

> "Let anyone who is thirsty come to me, and let the one who believes in me drink. As the scripture has said, 'Out of the believer's heart shall flow rivers of living water.' " (7:37-38).

The narrator goes on to make an explicit link between the water symbolism, the gift of the Spirit, and the death of Jesus:

> "Now this he said about the Spirit, which believers in him were to receive; for as yet there was no Spirit, because Jesus was not yet glorified" (7:39).

The use of this verse as the key to the water symbolism of 19:34 is, however, not a perfect fit. The precise meaning of 7:38 is unclear. The Greek text literally uses not *"believer's* heart," as the New Revised Standard translation states but uses an indefinite pronoun, *autou,* which could refer either to Jesus as the source of the Spirit (and, therefore, be translated as *"his* heart") or to the believer who is now embued with the Spirit, as the *New Revised Standard* prefers.[4]

If the verse is translated as the *New Revised Standard Version* does, with the streams of living water flowing from the heart of the one who believes in Jesus rather than from Jesus himself, then this verse does not match the symbolism of the water flowing from the side of Jesus on the cross.

However, one should not view the correspondance between these two symbolic moments in John too mechanically. Symbols usually have a plastic, supple quality. "Water" clearly has a symbolic meaning in John and is used to express the powerful new life that Jesus gives the believer. Furthermore, water is expressive of the Spirit in which the life-giving power of Jesus' death is experienced. These sure symbolic meanings for "water" in the Fourth Gospel enable the reader to infer the meaning of the flow of water from the open side of the crucified Jesus. That stream of water is no longer to be viewed as a hideous sign of death but, paradoxically, as sign of the life this death brings. On the literal level of the story, the lance thrust is intended to confirm the death of Jesus; on the symbolic level it confirms the saving power of that death. From the cross of Jesus the power of the Spirit of God flows out into the world.

Determining the precise meaning of the "blood" symbol is more challenging. One of the most striking and often cited parallels to 19:34 is found in the First Letter of John:

> "This is the one who came by water and blood, Jesus Christ, not with the water only but with the water and the blood. And the Spirit is the one that testifies, for the Spirit is the truth. There are three that testify: the Spirit and the water and the blood, and these three agree." (I John 5:6-8)

---

[4] See the discussion of the various possibilities in R. Brown, *The Gospel According to John I-XII*, 320–21; he prefers the so-called "christological intepretation" which sees Christ as the referent but acknowledges that both possibilities have a long history in the church and the text itself can support either translation. For a survey of ancient and contemporary interpretation of this text, see Sr. Thomas More, *His Witness is True: John and His Interpreters* (New York: Peter Lang, 1988).

There is a convergence here of the same elements found in the crucifixion scene: a reference to "water," "blood," and to testimony (see 19:35). The meaning of the passage in I John seems to be that all three witnesses—the presence of the Spirit, the baptism of Jesus (water), and the death of Jesus (blood)—testify to Jesus' identity as the Son of God (see I John 5:5, 9, 10). The Johannine community experiences this life-giving encounter with the Spirit and the power of Jesus' death in its sacramental life of baptism and eucharist.[5] The "blood" therefore is symbolic of the saving death of Jesus. Earlier in the letter, the author explicitly refers to the blood of Jesus in this fashion: ". . . but if we walk in the light, as he himself is in the light, we have fellowship with one another, and the blood of Jesus his Son cleanses us from all sin" (I John 1:7).

Using the First Letter of John to interpret the meaning of a passage in the Gospel does have some risks. Although the Gospel and the Johannine letters have strong affinity and come from the same tradition, we cannot be sure that they are using a symbol such as "blood" in a univocal way.

However, there is another use of "blood" in a symbolic fashion found in the Gospel itself that confirms its meaning as expressing the saving power of Jesus' death in 19:34. In the Bread of Life discourse of chapter six, there are five references to the "blood" of Jesus.[6] In each case the blood of Jesus brings life to those who receive it:

"Very truly, I tell you, unless you eat the flesh of the Son of Man and drink his blood, you have no life in you" (6:53).

"Those who eat my flesh and drink my blood have eternal life, and I will raise them up at the last day" (6:54).

"For my flesh is true food, and my blood is true drink. Those who eat my flesh and drink my blood abide in me, and I in them." (6:55-56).

---

[5] See R. Brown, *The Epistles of John* (AB 30; Garden City: Doubleday, 1982), 594–99; also, P. Perkins, *The Johannine Epistles* (New Testament Message 21; Wilmington: Michael Glazier, 1979), 60–62.

[6] The only other reference to "blood" in the Gospel is 1:13, describing the children of God who are born "not of bloods" i.e., not born in a merely human fashion by the mingling of bloods. This is of no significance for the meaning of "blood" in 19:34.

It is curious that many commentators appeal to the passage in the First Letter of John but seem to ignore any correspondance with the symbol of blood in chapter 6 of the Gospel.[7] But the parallels are too important to overlook. In the Bread of Life discourse, at the beginning of the section in which the references to "blood" are found, there is a clear allusion to the death of Jesus: "and the bread *that I will give for the life of the world* is my flesh" (6:51b). There is great debate among Johannine scholars whether this entire latter section of the discourse was added by a later redactor, and to what degree its apparent sacramental theology is integrated into the theology of the Fourth Gospel.[8] There is more consensus over the fact that the basic theme of the discourse, at least up to 6:51, has to do with faith in Jesus as the "Living Bread come down from heaven." The introduction of the symbolic and probably sacramental language of "eating" and "drinking" that predominates 6:51-59 builds on that faith motif, stressing vital contact with Jesus in the eating of his flesh and the drinking of his blood.

Although "flesh" and "blood" in chapter 6 form a couplet signifying the entire human entity of Jesus, it also seems plausible that the final redactor would link the "blood" of Jesus to his death. This is confirmed by 19:34 where the evangelist refers to the "blood" that flows from the open side of the crucified Jesus, a sign that provokes the dramatic testimony of 19:35. In chapter 6 both the flesh and the blood of Jesus give life to the believer; the same meaning is attached to the blood of Jesus in the First Letter of John. There is every reason to assume that the evangelist intends the same meaning in the only other reference to the blood of Jesus, namely that which is under consideration in 19:34.[9]

Therefore we can conclude that the flow of blood and water from the pierced side of Jesus signifies the salvific effects of Jesus' death. The death of Jesus, in John's perspective, has an immediate impact: the Spirit of God flows out into the world. This had

---

[7] See, for example, R. Kysar, *John,* 291–92, who discusses the possible symbolism without any reference to the meaning of "blood" within John's Gospel itself.

[8] See the state of the question in R. Brown, *The Gospel According to John I-XII,* 285–91.

[9] See M. Thompson, *The Humanity of Jesus,* 110.

been promised in Jesus' final discourse: "Nevertheless I tell you the truth: it is to your advantage that I go away, for if I do not go away, the Advocate will not come to you; but if I go, I will send him to you." (John 16:7). In a very true sense, the resurrection is anti-climatic for the Johannine tradition; his death on the cross signals the moment when Jesus completes his mission, returns in triumph to his Father, and lavishes the gift of the Spirit on the world.

Can one go beyond this basic interpretation and find a specific sacramental meaning in the symbols of blood and water? In other words, does the evangelist also imply that the sacraments of baptism (water) and eucharist (blood) find their root in the saving death of Jesus and become the means by which the believer encounters the power of the Spirit? Certainly "water" has baptismal connotations in the discourse with Nicodemus (see 3:5) and "blood" has eucharistic meaning in 6:53-56, but this does not insure that the same symbolic meaning carries over into the flow of blood and water from the side of Jesus (19:34). At best, we can say that a sacramental meaning would be a "secondary" level of symbolism in 19:34, quite probable but not certain.[10]

We come finally to the scripture quotation which the evangelist links to the piercing of Jesus' side: "And again another passage of scripture says, "They will look on the one whom they have pierced'" (19:37). Here, too, the precise meaning intended is elusive. The quote is from Zechariah 12:10 but the difficulty is in deciding what mood the evangelist wishes to draw from the text. Is the subject the enemies of Jesus? Or the soldiers who have executed him? Or is a broader audience intended, such as the disciples or the believers in Jesus? And what is the tenor of their "looking" at the one they have pierced?

The original citation from Zechariah speaks of the "inhabitants of Jerusalem" receiving compassion from God when they look on the martyred prophet or king and mourn his death:

[10] See a similar position in R. Brown, *The Gospel According to John XIII-XXI,* 950–52; on the entire issue of "sacraments" in John's Gospel, see B. Lindars, "Word and Sacrament in the Fourth Gospel," *Scottish Journal of Theology* 29 (1976) 49–63 and F. J. Moloney, "When is John Talking about Sacraments?" *Australian Biblical Review* 30 (1982) 10–33.

> "And I will pour out a spirit of compassion and supplication on the house of David and the inhabitants of Jerusalem, so that, when they look on the one whom they have pierced, they shall mourn for him, as one mourns for an only child, and weep bitterly over him, as one weeps over a firstborn." (Zechariah 12:10)

Given the tone of Zechariah 12:10 it is difficult to interpret the passage in John other than in a positive sense. Those who look on the crucified Jesus and see the flow of life-giving water and saving blood from his side will experience God's compassion. They will mourn the death of Jesus because it is the death of their Lord (as Mary Magdalene does in 20:13) but they will be saved by his ultimate act of love for the world. This was Jesus' promise in the Gospel, particularly in the "lifting up" sayings:

> "And just as Moses lifted up the serpent in the wilderness, so must the Son of Man be lifted up, that whoever believes in him may have eternal life" (3:14-15)

> "When you have lifted up the Son of Man, then you will realize that I am he, and that I do nothing on my own, but speak these things as the Father instructed me" (8:28)

> "Now is the judgment of this world; now the ruler of this world be driven out. And I, when I am lifted up from the earth, will draw all people to myself." (12:31-32).[11]

And this is what the witness in 19:35 affirms. The evangelist strongly punctuates this moment in the Passion narrative. The death of Jesus, its reality confirmed by the lance thrust and its salvific power displayed in the symbols of blood and water, is the ultimate revelation of the Gospel. This is what the witness "sees" and this becomes the basic content of the community's testimony. Through that testimony the recipients of the gospel will believe in Jesus and be saved. This unnamed "witness" is most probably the Beloved Disciple whose insight into Jesus is the foundation of the Johannine church and who was present at

---

[11] On the "lifting up" sayings, see above Part I, pp. 34–36.

the cross (19:26-27).[12] He is surely the forerunner of the mission of the Johannine church, a mission that will be explicitly entrusted to the disciples by the Risen Christ (see 20:21).

The ones who have pierced Jesus are his enemies—immediately the Roman executioners but through their agency the leaders and ultimately Israel itself. We cannot be sure, however, about the identity of the ones who gaze on the pierced Jesus: are they the same as the ones who have pierced Jesus, and is there, accordingly, a promise of compassion for them? Or does "they" refer first of all to the community representatives gathered at the cross—the women, the mother of Jesus, and the beloved disiple—and through them to all who will believe in the name of Jesus?

The latter possibility seems more plausible.[13] John draws a deep line between those who believe in Jesus and those who reject him. While the death of Jesus offers salvation to the whole world, the opponents of Jesus in the Gospel seemed fixed in their emnity and thereby have already led themselves to condemnation (see 3:18-21; 12:46-50).

V. Finale (19:38-42)

John's Passion narrative concludes with the brief burial scene. The majestic drama and laden symbolism of the preceding crucifixion account give the finale an anti-climactic mood. But John's stunning interpretation of Jesus and his death still lingers in the air of quiet triumph that follows the crucified Jesus to the grave.

The relationship of John's burial account to that of the Synoptics is problematic. Some details coincide with the Synoptic versions: the rapid burial in accord with Jewish custom; the presence of Joseph of Arimathea; use of a new rock hewn tomb. But other elements are unique to John: the inclusion of Nicodemus and the

---

[12] See, for example, C. K. Barrett, *The Gospel According to St. John,* 557-58R. R. Brown, *The Gospel According to John XIII-XXI,* 936-37; R. Schnackenburg, *The Gospel According to St. John,* vol. 3, 290-91; R. A. Culpepper, *Anatomy of the Fourth Gospel,* 122.

[13] See R. Schnackenburg, *The Gospel According to St. John,* vol. 3, 293-94; B. Lindars, *The Gospel of John,* 591; R. Brown, on the other hand, sees two levels of meaning, one negative and the other positive; see, *The Gospel According to John XIII-XXI,* 954-55.

absence of the women; the use of a massive amount of spices; the location of the tomb in a "garden." Particularly in these details specific to John does the evangelist's subtle interpretation of the scene become apparent.

> [19:38] After these things, Joseph of Arimathea, who was a disciple of Jesus, though a secret one because of his fear of the Jews, asked Pilate to let him take away the body of Jesus. Pilate gave him permission; so he came and removed his body. [39] Nicodemus, who had at first come to Jesus by night, also came, bringing a mixture of myrrh and aloes, weighing about a hundred pounds. [40] They took the body of Jesus and wrapped it with the spices in linen cloths, according to the burial custom of the Jews. [41] Now there was a garden in the place where he was crucified, and in the garden there was a new tomb in which no one had ever been laid. [42] And so, because it was the Jewish day of Preparation, and the tomb was nearby, they laid Jesus there.

JOSEPH AND NICODEMUS

Two new characters enter the drama of the Passion to care for the burial of the crucified Jesus. John introduces Joseph of Arimathea as a "disciple of Jesus" but one who was "though a secret one, because of his fear of the Jews" (19:38). The other is Nicodemus whose association with Jesus is also qualified: "who had at first come to Jesus by night" (19:39). The manner in which these two are introduced is evidence that John wishes to draw some meaning from their presence at the burial of Jesus. As is often the case with John's Gospel, however, the intended meaning is enticingly vague.

Both men are drawn to Jesus but previously did so only in a furtive manner. This is the only appearance of Joseph in the Gospel but the evangelist suggests a previous history with Jesus. Joseph was a "disciple" but a secret one because he feared reprisal from the Jewish authorities. Earlier in the Gospel, such a response by would-be disciples among the leaders themselves was harshly judged: "Nevertheless many, even of the authorities, believed in him. But because of the Pharisees they did not confess it, for fear that they should be put out of the synagogue; for they loved human glory more than the glory that comes from God'' (12:42-43). But in other instances such fear is noted merely as a sign of weakness or partial faith, as in the case of the ordinary people in 7:13, the parents of the blind man in 9:22, and the disciples themselves in 20:19.[1]

Nicodemus is one of the few minor characters of John's Gospel who makes several appearnces on stage in the course of the narrative. The characterization of him as one who had first come to Jesus "by night" brings the reader back to chapter three of the Gospel. Here Nicodemus was introduced as a "man of the Pharisees" and a "ruler of the Jews" (3:1), and one who comes "by night" because he is convinced that Jesus is a "teacher come from God" and that "God is with" Jesus (3:2). As significant as such declarations are, they fall short of a Johannine confession of faith, as the ensuing dialogue with Jesus makes clear. Nicodemus fails to understand the heavenly origin of Jesus and the possibility of rebirth that he opens to the world (3:9). His insufficient faith aligns him clearly with those leaders of Israel who do not receive Jesus' testimony and do not believe in him (3:11-12).

Thus Nicodemus' coming to Jesus "by night" takes on a symbolic meaning: he is mired in the darkness of misunderstanding and unbelief. John uses "night" and darkness with this meaning in his Gospel. At the conclusion of the discourse triggered by the conversation with Nicodemus, Jesus utters words of prophetic judgment on those who love "darkness rather than light because their deeds were evil. For all who do evil hate the light, so that their deeds may not be exposed." (3:19-20). At the beginning of the Passion story, John had marked the moment of Judas' treachery with the comment: "and it was night" (13:30).

Despite these harsh condemnations, there is reason to believe that John's Gospel does not view Nicodemus as a lost cause. He reappears in the drama in chapter 7 where he risks some exposure of his belief in Jesus. When officers sent by the Pharisees fail to

---

[1] Brown and others have suggested that this reflects actual circumstances in the Johannine Church in which some Jewish believers in Jesus did not reveal their faith openly for fear of reprisal; John's Gospel may be appealing to them for greater courage. See R. Brown, *The Community of the Beloved Disciple*, 71-73.

arrest Jesus because they, too, seem enthralled by his teaching ("Never has anyone spoken like this!" 7:46), the authorities are furious and accuse them of being led astray. At that tense moment, Nicodemus speaks, however cautiously, in Jesus' defense: "Our law does not judge people without first giving them a hearing to find out what they are doing (7:51).

Both characters then are ambiguous disciples at best: Joseph a secret disciple out of fear and Nicodemus still "one of them" (7:50) yet coming to Jesus in the night because he is intrigued by the power of his teaching. If John now means to present them in a more positive light, the clue has to be found in the burial scene itself, not in their previous history with Jesus.

Here, too, the signs are enticing but still somewhat ambiguous. As in the Synoptic accounts, it is Joseph who asks Pilate for the body of Jesus. In the sequence of John's story, this represents a clear intervention on Joseph's part. Earlier the Jews had asked Pilate to have the legs of the three crucified men broken and their bodies "taken away" so that the Sabbath and the Passover would not be violated (19:31). Pilate had granted the request and the soldiers were carrying out that command when they broke the legs of the two crucified with Jesus and lanced Jesus' side. Thus the act of Joseph is clearly presented as a public act. Although he previously had been a secret disciple of Jesus he now sheds his fear and publicly proclaims his allegiance by coming forward to claim the body in order to give it the honor of a proper burial. As the rest of the narrative shows, Joseph (and Nicodemus) intend this to truly honor Jesus.

Nicodemus, too, seems to have a turn of heart. The one who *"at first"* had come only by night, now "comes" publicly to offer extraordinary homage to Jesus, bringing a staggering amount of spices to honor his crucified body (19:39). The "mixture" of myrrh and aloes weighs literally 100 "litras," a Roman measure equal to 11:5 ounces, thus the total weight of the spices brought by Nicodemus is more than 70 pounds.

What is Nicodemus' intent? For those who believe that Nicodemus remains a negative character in the Gospel, this lavish amount of burial spices simply confirms that Nicodemus did not understand Jesus and his destiny. This Jewish teacher remains an unbeliever, unable to comprehend the fact that the crucified Jesus will burst from the tomb in triumph and has no need of protecting his mortal flesh from corruption.[2] But others see Nicodemus' homage in a more positive light. The extraordinary amount of spices suggests a royal burial for Jesus, extending the theme of royal triumph over death that was so strong in John's crucifixion narrative.[3] The placing of Jesus' body in a "new" and never before used tomb complements this royal motif (see 19:41).

Although John's portrayal of these characters is subtle, it seems likely that he considers them as emerging disciples, drawn into the light by the power that streams from the open side of Jesus. The key is the clearly public nature of claiming Jesus' body and honoring it in such an extraordinary way. John's issue with these two men was not the content of their belief in Jesus (e.g., his promise of resurrection), but their fear and hesitation in making their allegiance to Jesus public. The inevitably public dynamics in John's account of the burial—claiming the body of Jesus from Pilate, openly offering homage to a crucified criminal, burying him in a new tomb—are signs that Joseph was shedding his fear and Nicodemus was being drawn into the light. The prophetic declaration of Jesus about the magnetic power of his death was coming true: "And I, when I am lifted up from the earth, will draw all people to myself" (12:32). John's Gospel, along with the other New Testament accounts, is capable of describing these turning points with subtle accents. Resurrection faith seems to come as an awakening from a deep sleep: the responses are at first sluggish and partial but they are signs of surging new life. Such would be the experience of Simon, Mary, Thomas, and the entire corps of disciples in the resurrection appearance stories of chapter 20.[4]

---

[2] See, for example, D. Sylva, "Nicodemus and His Spices (Jn 19:39)," *New Testament Studies* 34 (1988) 148–51; similarly, R. A. Culpepper, *Anatomy of the Fourth Gospel*, 136; G. Nicholson, *Death as Departure*, 65–66; P. Duke, *Irony in the Fourth Gospel*, 110; D. Rensburger, *Johannine Faith and Liberating Community*, 40.

[3] See, for example, R. Brown, *The Gospel According to John XIII-XXI*, 959–60, who notes the large amount of spices interred with Herod according to Josephus' account and other later Jewish texts; see, also, R. Schnackenburg, *The Gospel According to St. John*, vol. 3, 296–97.

[4] See below, pp. 135–43. J. Bassler believes John's Gospel is deliberately "ambiguous" in its portrayal of Nicodemus, thereby inviting the reader to ponder Nicodemus' suspension between fear and commitment and to complete the story in their own lives through the com-

PREPARATION FOR EASTER

In some ways, John's burial scene has a more pronounced finality than its Synoptic parallels.[5] There are no women present to note the place of burial and then to come after the Sabbath to anoint the body (see Mk 15:47–16:1-2 and the parallel passages in Matthew and Luke). In John the burial of Jesus' body took place by anticipation at Bethany (12:1-8), and even though that narrative seems to anticipate a later burial anointing by Mary (12:7), it will not take place. The aromatic spices wrapped in the burial cloths also may be seen by John as part of Jesus' burial anointing. Nor, as in the Synoptics, does the device of rolling the stone to seal the entrance prepare for the explosive force of an empty tomb with its rock rolled back by angelic powers.

Nevertheless, John's story, too, has resurrection in mind as it narrates the ritual of death and burial. The royal motif implicit in the amount of spices and the homage by previously hesitant disciples is one indicator of this. So, too, are more subtle links to the wondrous events of chapter 20. Jesus' body is bound in "linen cloths" (19:40), and those same burial garments will be spotted by Simon Peter as the stupefied disciple enters the empty tomb on Easter morning (20:6-7). The tomb is located in a "garden," (19:41), a detail that evokes memories of another "garden" where the Passion drama began (18:1). Mary Magdalene, the first in John's Gospel to witness the Risen Christ, will stand weeping near the empty tomb and mistakenly suppose that the Risen Jesus is the "gardener" (20:15).[6]

Finally, the haste of Jesus' burial prevents the scene from being completely conclusive. Jesus is buried in the newly cut tomb because it was "close by" and because the beginning of the Sabbath and the feast was imminent (19:42). The story ends on an uncertain note of haste and improvisation. But John's deft ironic

mitment of discipleship; see, "Mixed Signals: Nicodemus in the Fourth Gospel," *Journal of Biblical Literature* 4 (1989) 635–46.

[5] See the remarks of R. Schnackenburg, *The Gospel According to St. John,* vol. 3, 297; J. T. Forestell, *The Word of the Cross,* 92.

[6] Some have suggested the possibility that John's reference to a "garden" has symbolic meaning, perhaps evoking the garden of eden; see the discussion in R. Brown, *The Gospel According to John XIII-XXI,* 943. But, if present, such an allusion is extraordinarily subtle on the evangelist's part.

touch shows once more. The burial of Jesus can be hasty and incomplete because a stronger, deeper force rules his destiny. The reader knows that this tomb will not be the final resting place of the one who is Resurrection and Life.

VI. Triumph over Death: The Resurrection Appearances (John 20:1–21:25)

While the Passion narrative commands our focus, it is also useful to trace how John follows through on his portrayal of Jesus' death in recounting the Easter events. None of the canonical Gospels attempts to describe the resurrection itself; instead we see the powerful impact of Jesus' triumph on his disciples.

John narrates four appearances of the Risen Christ, three of them in Jerusalem and one in Galilee. Two take place on the Sunday immediately after the death of Jesus and one other the week following. The timing of the Galilean appearance is left vague ("After these things . . ."). These incidents find some echo in the Synoptic Gospels but each carries its distinctive Johannine stamp.

DISCOVERY OF THE EMPTY TOMB (20:1-10)

As in the Synoptic Gospels, the first proclamation of Jesus' triumph over death comes through the discovery of the empty tomb.[1] The evangelist had prepared the reader for this scene in the immediately preceding burial account (19:38-42). Joseph and Nicodemus wrap the body of the Crucified in linen cloths and place him in a new tomb. The burial is done with some haste because it was "the Jewish Day of Preparation" (19:42).

The Sabbath rest is over and on "the first day of the week"— what will ultimately become the Christian day of prayer—Mary Magdalene comes to the tomb. In the Synoptic Gospels the women come to anoint Jesus, an important Jewish act of reverence for the dead that was left undone in the haste of his burial. But Jesus' body had been lavishly anointed in John's version (19:39-40), so Mary's reason for coming is presumably her heartache for Jesus.

[1] See Mark 16:1-8 and the parallels in Matthew 28:1-10 and Luke 24:1-12.

Mary Magdalene made her first appearance in John's Gospel at the crucifixion; she, along with other women and the Beloved Disciple stood near the cross during Jesus' final agony. John gives us no information about Mary. Taking its cue from Luke's description of her as someone "from whom seven demons had gone out" (Lk 8:2), popular tradition from ancient times until recent Hollywood versions, has portrayed Mary as a reformed prostitute. But, in fact, Luke's description could simply mean she had been delivered from an extremely virulent disease.[2] In any case, she will be the key witness to the resurrection in John's narrative.[3]

When she discovers the tomb empty, she runs to tell the disciples. Two very familiar Johannine characters now enter the drama: Simon Peter and the Beloved Disciple. Mary's first reaction to the empty tomb is to conclude that grave robbers had taken the body of Jesus (20:2). It will be up to the Beloved Disciple, always the model in John's perspective, to understand what has really happened.[4] The two disciples run to the tomb togther, but again consistent with John's point of view, the Beloved Disciple shines. He runs more swiftly than Peter and, without entering the tomb, observes the burial cloth and the neatly wrapped face covering, details that evoke the raising of Lazarus who emerges from the tomb bound in a shroud and his face "wrapped in a cloth" (11:44).[5] Peter enters the tomb first but does not yet react. When the Beloved Disciple enters, he "saw and believed" (20:8).

The scene's concluding comment is somewhat enigmatic, presumably applying to Mary and Peter at this point: "for as yet they did not understand the scripture, that he must rise from the dead" (20:9). The triumph of resurrection has constantly shimmered through John's narration of the Passion story. There is, in a sense, little need to convince the reader of Jesus' victory over

---

[2] See E. Moltmann-Wendel, *The Women Around Jesus* (New York: Crossroad, 1982), 61–92.

[3] On the role of women in John, see R. Brown's "Roles of Women in the Fourth Gospel," *Theological Studies* 36 (1975) 688–99, and more recently, S. Schneider, "Women in the Fourth Gospel and the Role of Women in the Contemporary Church," *Biblical Theology Bulletin* 12 (1982) 35–45.

[4] See above, pp. 63–64.

[5] The Greek word *soudarion* is used in both instances. On the importance of the Lazarus story for John's interpretation of the death of Jesus, see above, Part I, pp. 32–33.

death. The intent of these stories, rather, is to show how that triumph gradually transforms the fear and hesitation of the community.

THE APPEARANCE TO MARY MAGDALENE (20:11-18).

This beautiful story, filled with Johannine touches, relates the first appearance of Jesus. The Risen Christ first reveals himself not to the disciples but to Mary Magdalene.

Mary is grief stricken because she remains convinced that someone has stolen the body of Jesus. Still weeping, she bends over and looks into the tomb. What she sees are two angels, dressed in white, marking the place where Jesus' body had lain. Even this astounding apparition seems unable to penetrate her grief; that is reserved for Jesus himself. She turns around and sees Jesus standing there, but does not recognize him.[6] He poses the same question the angels had: "Woman, why are you weeping?" but adds the kind of open ended question so typical of the Gospel: "Whom are you looking for?."[7] She is still fixed in her hopeless conviction that the grave of Jesus has been violated and that someone has taken his body (20:15). Only when Jesus says her name—"Mary"—does she suddenly realize the incredible truth of his presence: "Rabbouni!" (20:16).

That exquisite moment transforms grief to faith. But Jesus' triumph over death has brought a new and decisive era in history. Mary is not to cling to Jesus because he is about to complete his triumphant mission by ascending to his Father, "to my God and your God" (20:17). The great farewell prayer of Jesus in chapter 17 had revealed to the disciples that union with God was the endpoint of Jesus' mission. Having passed triumphantly through the portals of death, Jesus would now enter into his life with God.

The announcement of that full triumph of Jesus is entrusted to Mary; she, in effect, becomes the first missionary of the Johannine church. Charged with resurrection faith she goes to the disciples and makes her dramatic announcement: "I have seen the Lord!" (20:18).

[6] This is a typical motif in the gospel resurrection appearance stories, expressing the new mode of existence associated with resurrection: e.g., Luke 24:16, 37; John 21:4.

[7] See the examples cited above, p. 51.

THE FIRST APPEARANCE TO THE DISCIPLES (20:19-23)

Another story of transformation takes place, this time involving the disciples as a whole (with the exception of Thomas). The disciples huddle in a house "for fear of the Jews" (20:19). The Fourth Gospel continues to portray the opponents in stereotyped negative tones, as implacably hostile to Jesus and his community.[8]

The Risen Jesus breaks into this circle of fear, greeting the disciples with a greeting of peace and showing them the wounds in his hands and side (20:19-20). "Peace" was a gift of the endtime; its realization comes now through the transforming power of Jesus' triumphant death. Displaying Jesus' wounds is another multi-layered Johannine sign. Those marks of death confirm for the disciples that the living being they see before them is, indeed, the same Jesus they knew. They are also paradoxical signs of triumph; through his crucifixion Jesus had proclaimed God's love for the world and triumphed over the powers of darkness. From his open side had flowed blood and water, signs of the life that would now pour out into the world (19:34).[9]

The power of Jesus' death is confirmed in the reaction of the disciples. They "rejoiced when they saw the Lord" (20:20). On them Jesus lavishes the gift of the Spirit and and the power of reconciliation. He sends them out into the world to continue his own mission, "sent as he is sent." This scene, in effect, is the commission of the disciples, equivalent in Johannine terms, to the mission entrusted to the disciples by the Risen Christ in Luke 24:36-49 and confirmed in the experience of Pentecost (Acts 2), or the mission charge to the disciples given by the triumphant Son of Man in the concluding mountaintop scene of Matthew's Gospel (Mt 28:16-20).

THE APPEARANCE TO THOMAS (20:24-31)

This incident makes clear what has been implicit in each of the previous appearances. The Gospel's interest is not riveted on the past but on the future—on the transformation to be experienced

---

[8] See above, Part I, pp. 39-42.
[9] See the discussion of this text, above, pp. 121-29.

by those who believe in Jesus yet without the privilege of knowing him in the flesh. Thomas, the disciple who insists on touching Jesus, illustrates the Gospel's conviction that faith in Jesus is by no means restricted to the golden age of the first disciples or to those who witnessed his resurrection appearances.

Thomas' declaration once again draws attention to the triumphant wounds of Jesus: he must "see" and "touch" the marks of the nails in his hands and put his hand "in his side" (20:25). The Sunday following the first appearnce, Thomas is granted his wish. Once again Jesus mysteriously enters the locked house of the disciples and greets them with the greeting of peace. He moves immediately to Thomas and invites him to touch his hands and side.

As is the case with each of these experiences, the presence of the Risen Christ makes a difference. Thomas' aggressive doubt dissolves into vigorous faith: "My Lord and my God"—one of the Gospel's most profound confessions of Jesus' true identity.

But the story's true interest is in the future, in the generations of believers who cannot touch the wounds of Jesus. Thomas believes because he "sees"; Jesus blesses those "who have not seen and yet have come to believe" (20:29). Typical of the multi-layered possibilities of meaning so favored by the evangelist, the notion of "seeing" has many levels of meaning in John.[10] In some instances to "see" means an insistence on proof, on tactile, visible supports for faith (e.g., 6:2; 20:25). At other times, however, it is the prelude to faith, as was the case with the Beloved Disciple's "seeing" the burial cloths and the empty tomb (20:8), or Mary Magdalene finally recognizing Jesus when he speaks her name (20:14-16), and, of course, Thomas himself whose faith is stirred when he is invited to verify the nail prints in Jesus' hands and touch the wound on his side.

But John's community was already in a different generation; time had taken from their circle those early followers who could say, as Mary had, "I have seen the Lord" (20:18). Their "seeing" had to be of a different variety, the penetrating insight of faith granted by the power of the Spirit, the Paraclete, and ig-

---

[10] R. Kysar, *John: The Maverick Gospel*, 73-77; C. Koester, "Hearing, Seeing, and Believing in the Gospel of John," *Biblica* 70 (1989) 327-48.

nited by the preaching of the Word. For these Jesus had prayed on the evening before his death: "I ask not only on behalf of these (disciples), but also on behalf of those who will believe in me through their word." (17:20). Jesus' final instruction to his disciples is that this experience of faith "without seeing" is no less authentic, no less life-giving than that of the first generation of believers.

The concluding words of chapter 20 seem to ring down the curtain on the entire Gospel story.

> "Now Jesus did many other signs in the presence of his disciples, which are not written in this book. But these are written so that you may come to believe that Jesus is the messiah, the Son of God, and that through believing you may have life in his name." (20:30-31).

The finality of these words has led many interpreters to conclude that at one stage in the Gospel's formation, this was the ending of the Gospel, thus making chapter 21 a later appendage.[11] Whether an original ending or an anti-climactic summary, the verses reveal a purpose for the Gospel already quite evident to the reader. Jesus' glorious signs, only a few of which are included in the narrative, are to lead their witnesses to faith. This was the impact on the disciples themselves. In seeing Jesus' signs with the eyes of faith they came to believe that he was the Messiah and the Son of God. The endpoint of faith—indeed of Jesus' entire mission—was that through faith the believer would experience everlasting life.

The reader who has just completed the story of the death of Jesus and savored the joy and triumph of the empty tomb knows that the greatest and most faith-provoking sign of all is the sign of the cross.[12]

---

[11] See discussion in R. Brown, *The Gospel According to John XIII-XXI*, 1077-82.

[12] C. H. Dodd's comment is most apt: ". . . we can hardly fail to see that the motives of a whole series of *semeia* [signs] are gathered up in this supreme *semeion* [i.e., the death of Jesus]: the sign of the wine of Cana, which we now perceive to be the blood of the true Vine; the sign of the Temple (which is the Body of Christ) destroyed to be raised again; the signs of the life-giving word (at Cana and Bethesda) since the Word Himself is life and dies that men may be saved from death; the sign of the Bread, which is the flesh of Christ given for

THE APPEARANCE AT THE SEA OF TIBERIAS AND THE DESTINIES OF SIMON PETER AND THE BELOVED DISCIPLE (21:1-25)

Just as John's drama appears to conclude triumphantly, another reel starts up. The scene shifts from Jerusalem to Galilee where the disciples have gathered; once again the Risen Jesus will come mysteriously into their lives.

While it is likely that this resurrection appearance story of chapter 21 is a "supplement" to the Gospel, its close connections with the preceding narrative and the theology of the Fourth Gospel as a whole should not be overlooked. This chapter takes up a key issue that has woven its way through the Gospel, including the Passion: what are the roles and destiny in the post-Easter church of the two most prominent followers of Jesus—Simon Peter and the Beloved Disciple?

The appearance of Jesus to his disciples at the Sea is a tender mood piece, one of the New Testament's most memorable stories. If this episode was written later and by another hand than the scenes in chapter 20, it certainly takes into account these earlier appearances. Prominent among those who gather at the lake are Simon Peter, Thomas, and, of course, the Beloved Disciple—the chief male characters in chapter 20. The impact of Jesus' resurrection, however, seems to have dulled; the disciples who had been empowered for mission by the Risen Christ (20:21) return to their former life as fishermen (21:3). After a night on the sea, they catch nothing. The scene is heavy with disappointment and listless failure.

As it did in Jerusalem, the sudden and mysterious appearance of the Risen Jesus at daybreak transforms the disciples. Before

the life of the world; the sign of Lazarus—life victorious over death through the laying down of life; the sign of the anointing for burial; and the sign of the "King of Israel" acclaimed on His entry to Jerusalem to die. Along with these, other symbols, which although they have not been embodied in dramatic incidents have been woven into the discourses, have their significance clarified and enhanced in this supreme *semeion:* Moses' serpent (the sign of salvation), living water, the good shepherd, the grain of wheat, the woman in travail. As everywhere, so most emphatically in the story of Christ's arrest, trial and crucifixion, what happens and is observed in the temporal and sensible sphere signified eternal reality: the life eternal given to man through the eternal Word. In this sense the Passion of the Lord is the final and all-inclusive *semeion." The Interpretation of the Fourth Gospel* (Cambridge: Cambridge University Press, 1953), 438-39.

they even recognize him, he directs them to a tremendous catch. As before, it is the Beloved Disciple who first recognizes Jesus and informs Simon Peter (21:7).

The evangelist blends into this episode a motif favored by Luke.[13] The Risen Christ prepares a meal of fish and bread over charcoals, breaking the bread and giving it to the disciples—a scene that evokes the Eucharist and the wondrous meal of the Risen Christ with the disciples at Emmaus (Luke 24:13-35).

But John's real interest does not linger at the meal. The spotlight falls on Peter. Simon's threefold denial of Jesus during the Passion is still a fresh wound, perhaps soothed a bit by the appearances in Jerusalem but until now never resolved by the Gospel (see 18:15-18, 25-27). The Risen Jesus draws from the disciple a threefold declaration of love, each question of Jesus painfully healing Peter's broken bond with his Master. But reconciliation with Peter is not the final step; the Risen Jesus empowers him to pastor the community. He is to "tend" and "feed" the sheep, assuming the mantle of the Good Shepherd that Jesus himself had borne (10:1-17).

Peter, in other words, is given pastoral leadership in the community. That responsibility may already have been symbolized in the great catch of fish the disciples had landed with Jesus' guidance and which Peter had been instructed to haul ashore (21:8-11). The significance of the great catch—153 large fish—surely is an augur of the expansive mission of the community, although the precise meaning of "153" has eluded commentators for centuries.[14] Thus Peter is to be immmersed in the community's mission and to care for the community's life—two crucial dimensions of pastoral leadership that Jesus himself had exemplified in the Gospel.

There was one more share in Jesus' destiny left for Peter. Like his master, Peter would go "where he did not want to go"— through the experience of violent death for the sake of the Gospel (21:18-19). Jesus had already promised the disciple this destiny on the eve of his own Passion: "Where I am going, you cannot

---

[13] On the meal motif in Luke, see D. Senior, *The Passion of Jesus in the Gospel of Luke,* 156–57, and R. Karris, *Luke: Artist and Theologian* (New York: Paulist, 1985), 47–78.

[14] See, R. Brown, *The Gospel According to John XIII-XXI,* 1074–76.

follow me now; but you will follow afterward." (13:36). At that moment, Peter's bravado kept him from truly realizing what the cost of discipleship was: "Lord, why can I not follow you now? I will lay down my life for you." Jesus answered, "Will you lay down your life for me? Very truly, I tell you, before the cock crows, you will have denied me three times." (13:37-38).

His self-knowledge tempered by failure and the broken bonds of his discipleship cauterized by a threefold avowal of love, Peter is now ready to assume his mission and face his destiny with Jesus.

Now that the evangelist has dealt with the fate of Peter, only one question remains: what about the Beloved Disciple? The text seems to fend off a question that had apparently rippled through the community at the time of the Beloved Disciple's death. Jesus had never said that the Beloved Disciple "would not die" but only that his destiny was in the Lord's hands.

If Peter was entrusted with pastoral leadership in the community, the Gospel reserves for the Beloved Disciple an even more fundamental task. As had been the case throughout John's story, the Beloved Disciple is the privileged witness, the one who truly knows Jesus and gives authentic testimony to the community (21:24).

Thus Peter and the Beloved Disciple remain a special pair in this Gospel, during the ministry of Jesus and into the life of the community. John does not diminish Peter's role but there is no doubt that the Beloved Disciple has pride of place. The testimony of this disciple whom Jesus loved links the community to very Word of God.

The volume finally turns its last page with the summary statement of 21:24-25. The narrator stands back from the story that has unfolded from the encounter with the Baptist at the Jordan to the breakfast with the Risen Christ on the shore of Lake Tiberias. Those compelling scenes were only a small sample of the wondrous works done by Jesus, only a few words of the One whose love could fill the universe.

PART III

THE PASSION OF JESUS: JOHN'S MESSAGE

As stated from the outset of our study, the Passion narrative stands as a culmination of major themes of the Gospel. Having looking closely at the brushstrokes in John's portrayal of the Passion of Jesus, we are now ready to step back and take in the canvas as a whole. Our point is not to restate the major lines of John's theology (see Part I) but to summarize the way they come to term in the Passion of Jesus.

I. The Passion and John's Portrayal of Jesus

Through the Passion John's Gospel proclaims that the death of Jesus, as an act of total self-donation, is the ultimate revelation of God's redemptive love for the world.

Presenting Jesus as the revelation of God is the hallmark of Johannine theology. The fundamental thesis of John's Gospel is that every facet of Jesus' existence—his person, his mission, his destiny—reveals who God is and what is God's stance toward the world.[1] John mobilizes a whole range of metaphors, symbols, and events to affirm this understanding of Jesus. Accordingly, John describes the cosmic mission of Jesus as the "Word" incarnate who brings God's message of love to a stricken world.[2] That "word" of God is expressed in multiple ways—through Jesus'

---

[1] See the discussion of this theme in Part I, pp. 16–18.

[2] See above, pp. 16–17.

signs of power and compassion; through his electrifying discourses; and in the bold commitments of his life and mission. Indeed, Jesus bears the very name of God, "I Am."[3] His word is "truth" because his person and his mission reveal the ultimate truth of God. His testimony is trustworthy and his actions are the very work of God.

For John's Gospel, no "word" of Jesus is more eloquent, no sign more transparent, no testimony more compelling than that of his death. Even before the Passion begins to unfold, the Johannine Jesus had clearly interpreted his impending death as an act of love. Jesus was the "son" delivered by God out of love for the world (3:16-17). Jesus was the "Good Shepherd" who would lay down his life for his sheep (10:11); The "grain of wheat" that had to fall to the earth and die in order to bear fruit (12:24). Jesus was the singular friend who would give his very life out of love for his beloved (15:13). Jesus, indeed, would love his own "to the end" (13:1).

The Passion story is driven by this vision of the Gospel and several of its key features are shaped by it. Jesus' care for his disciples—his friends—comes through, for example, in the unique Johannine narration of the arrest. Jesus protects his disciples, allowing them to go free while he himself freely submits to the violence of Judas and the soldiers who come to seize him (18:8). The same care is at least part of the meaning of the final act of Jesus' life when he tends to his mother and the disciple "whom he loved" (19:26-27).

As the brutal drama of the trial and crucifixion takes its course, the evangelist harkens back to the themes of Jesus as revealer. Thus during his interrogation, Jesus challenges the High Priest: "I have spoken openly to the world; I have always taught in synagogues and in the temple, where all the Jews come together. I have said nothing in secret." (18:20). And he boldly tells an uncomprehending and spiritually dull Pilate that his entire destiny is to reveal the "truth" of God's love: "For this I was born, and for this I came into the world, to testify to the truth. Everyone who belongs to the truth listens to my voice." (18:37). Neither

---

[3] See above, p. 52.

the religious leaders nor the Roman ruler can comprehend that God's living truth and eternal Word stand embodied before them in their Galilean prisoner.

But the most powerful affirmation of Jesus' identity as God's word of love for the world comes not in specific metaphors or sayings of the Passion story but in the very dramatization of its climax, the death scene. The attentive reader of John's Gospel already knows the interpretation Jesus himself has given his death: it is an act of friendship love; it is a laying down of life for another; it is loving someone to the very end. The summit of John's Passion story has a bold, dramatic quality to it. As the Roman trial builds in tension, Pilate brings Jesus, flogged and crowned with mock symbols of power, outside to display him to the crowd—an apparent attempt to gain the crowd's pity and so release this haunting prisoner (19:5). But the reader—tuned to the subtle counterpoints of John's irony—realizes that this is not a display of pitiful defeat, but an ikon of love, Jesus the Incarnate "Word," truly a "man," a human being, but in the very act of giving up freedom and life enacting the ultimate and unimpeachable sign of love.

The crucifixion that follows adds further luminous layers of color to the Johannine portrait. Jesus is stripped of his garments, stripped of his dignity, stripped of his freedom and nailed to a cross. But once again John's palette is dipped in irony. The reader knows that the cross is really a cosmic stage on which the Son of Man will be "lifted up" for all the world to see (12:32). The Roman governor, attempting to sting the leaders, his victorious antagonists, writes Jesus' name and title in the languages of the world so that all who pass by can understand (19:20).

As death tightens its grip, Jesus himself knows that this is the "hour," the moment of truth when all of the work he had set out to do was now "completed," the cup he had longed to drink, the full measure of all of the love he intended to express until the very "finish" (19:28).[4] And in John's exquisite portrayal, Jesus dies with that declaration on his lips: "It is finished" (19:30). The Word was spoken; life given; love expressed. Jesus' work as the

---

[4] On the significance of this word in John, see above, pp. 115–20.

revealer of the true character of the biblical God had reached its successful conclusion.

By so profoundly transforming the meaning of the cross from an instrument of grisly death to a sign of overwhelming love, John's Gospel captures the inherent paradox of the Christian revelation and discloses the endless mystery of God's love for the world.

The death of Jesus is the victorious culmination of Jesus' mission, the "hour of glory" triumphantly leading him back to God.

Strangely, there is an air of triumph and victory in John's telling of the Passion story. Although it is, in fact, a narrative about a public execution—one prepared for by a nightime arrest, interrogations, beatings and torture—and even though it ends with death on a cross and a hasty burial in a stranger's tomb, the reader cannot miss the sense of triumph that surges through this story. This quality is far more pronounced in John's Gospel than it is in the Synoptic versions and it can be traced to the theology that underpins John's presentation of the death of Jesus.

Some of that theology is reflected in the theme we have described above. Because the death of Jesus is interpreted by John as an act of redeeming love, the Passion cannot be a tragedy. In similar fashion, the Johannine Jesus has spoken of his impending death as an hour of "glory" in that God's presence would be manifest to the world through the infinite tenderness of Jesus' love and through the power of his triumph over evil.[5]

Another expression of this basic theme of Jesus as revealer of God is the casting of death as a "return" to God. As we noted in Part I, John conceives of the overall mission of Jesus in "spatial" terms: the Word springs forth from God and comes "into the world," becoming flesh and abiding in human history.[6] Accordingly, the Gospel can also speak of Jesus' death as a "return" to God, as a "homecoming" in which Jesus goes back to the Father who sent him and abides forever in God's love.[7] The

[5] See above, pp. 36–39.

[6] See above, pp. 34–36.

[7] See above, p. 28.

destiny of Jesus foreshadows that of all believers; in his final testament, Jesus prays, "Father, I desire that those also, whom you have given me, may be with me where I am, to see my glory, which you have given me because you loved me before the foundation of the world." (17:24).

Here is another profound transformation of symbols. Instead of viewing death as a termination, a stopping of the flow of life, the Gospel portrays Jesus' death as a glorious beginning, as a portal through which Jesus passes from this world to the next, a homecoming into the loving arms of his God. Thus does Jesus complete his mission.

That sense of triumph hangs in the air of the entire Passion story. Jesus does not have the manner of a defeated man. He confronts his captors, driving them to their knees when he utters his divine name (18:6). He does not hesitate to challenge the High Priest (18:20-21, 23) and the Roman Governor (19:11) or to maintain an imperious and condemning silence in the face of their threats or pleas (19:9). When Pilate and his soldiers mock Jesus' claims to kingship, the reader knows that the crown and royal title fit Jesus (19:5). Even the dreaded ritual of crucifixion takes on a strangely victorious beat: Jesus carries his own cross to Golgotha (19:17); his crucifixion becomes an enthronement with an entourage on his right and his left (19:18); a proclamation of his royalty is pinned to the summit of his cross throne. And Jesus dies not with a cry of lament as in Mark and Matthew, nor even with a prayer of surrender as in Luke, but with assurance: "It is completed" (19:30). Even beyond the boundary of death, that sense of triumph continues as Jesus' body is spared the shattering of his legs and the lance thrust draws out a spring of blood and water, signs of new life (19:34).[8] And Jesus is buried with signs of royal homage (19:39).

For John's Gospel, the cross of Jesus becomes the portal to full life with God and thus the evangelist's impulse for allowing the victory of Jesus over death to lie so close to the surface of his narrative. Jesus does not enter a dread world but returns to God: "But now I am coming to you, and I speak these things in the world, so that they may have my joy made complete in themselves." (17:13).

[8] See below, pp. 157-59.

From his cross Jesus stands in judgment over the powers of dark-
ness and death and defeats them; at the same time the power of
the cross becomes a norm of judgment on all other expressions
of power.

As we noted from the outset, John's Gospel portrays Jesus in
constant conflict with those who misunderstand, reject, or oppose his mission.[9] This quality of the Gospel is an expression of
the evangelist's theological vision. The figure of Jesus is so overwhelming and the truth of his mission so transparent that response
is compelled: one either accepts Jesus and believes his word, or
disbelieves and rejects him. Because of Jesus' identity as the incarnate Word of God, all life rides on accepting his testimony.
To reject Jesus, therefore, ultimately means turning away from
life and choosing eternal death. Endorsing such a choice, in John's
perspective, can only be traced to the power of the demonic which
underwrites all of the opposition to Jesus.

John's christology, in other words, is a high stakes christology. Everything depends on Jesus and his Word of truth. As we
will note below, there is some relief from this dualistic stance in
his portrayal of such characters as Nicodemus and Peter, but for
the most part, the Gospel deals with absolutes: belief or unbelief;
light or darkness; life or death.[10]

The clash between Jesus and the power of evil comes to term
in the Passion story. Here the furies which lashed at him during
his ministry merge into a final assault against God's Word. That
merger is signaled in the opening scene when the fallen disciple,
Judas, guards from the Pharisees and the Chief Priests, and
Roman soldiers all band together to seize Jesus (18:3).

The opposition to Jesus took many forms in the Gospel and
each of them are represented in the Passion. Certainly the religious leaders whom John often merges into a stereotyped wall
of opposition—the "Jews"—are one virulent expression of disbelief in the Gospel.[11] In the Passion story they play a major role.
Their representatives are present for the arrest (18:3). Both the

---

[9] See above, pp. 39–42.

[10] See below, pp. 159–63.

[11] See below, pp. 155–57.

chief priest Caiaphas and his predecessor, Annas, hostilely interrogate Jesus (18:19-24), and, afterwards, the Jewish leaders turn
him over to Pilate for condemnation (18:28).

Throughout John's presentation of the Roman trial, the
leaders—usually labelled the "Jews"—remain unflinching protagonists, injecting new accusations against Jesus (19:7), badger-
ing Pilate (18:30; 19:12) and rejecting his weak attempts at
clemency (18:38-40; 19:4-7; 19:12; 19:14-15). Even as Jesus is executed, the "chief priests" protest the wording of the placard Pilate mounts over the cross (19:21). The depth of the leaders'
disbelief is measured by the astounding claims of allegiance they
make to Caesar in order to insure Jesus' condemnation. They warn
Pilate he will be "no friend of Caesar" if he releases Jesus for
"one who claims to be a king sets himself against the emperor"
(19:12) and finally go so far as to violate their own tradition by
declaring: "We have no king but the emperor" (19:15).

Most of the disciples are taken off stage early in the Passion
because Jesus protects them at the moment of his arrest and insures their safety—a sign of his role as the true Shepherd (18:8-9).[12]
But Judas, the fallen disciple, is infected with disbelief.[13] The al-
lure of darkness brings this tragic figure to the side of disbelief
so that he ends up leading the band of guards and soldiers who
come to arrest Jesus (18:2-3, 5). In the Passion story itself the
evangelist does not speculate any further on the fate of Judas;
that has already been dealt with in earlier scenes of the Gospel.
In his final prayer, Jesus declares that he had guarded from destruction all of those whom the Father had given him—except one,
"the one destined to be lost" (17:12).

In his denials of Jesus Peter will veer to the edge of the chasm
but will not be consumed. As we will discuss below, Peter is not
an example of disbelief in John's Gospel, but one of the rarer
examples of those who struggle in faith.[14]

Pilate is another Johannine character who, at first, seems to
have an ambiguous role in the Passion story. At the beginning
of the Roman trial Pilate stands in opposition to the Jews and

---

[12] See above, p. 53.

[13] On role of Judas in John, see above, pp. 48–53.

[14] See below, pp. 160–63.

supports Jesus. Four times he rebuffs their accusations (18:31, 38; 19:4, 6) and openly seeks the release of Jesus (18:39-40; 19:12). But as the trial unfolds it becomes clear that Pilate, too, is in a position of unbelief and that his efforts to release Jesus are motivated not by faith but by contempt for the Jews and by fear. At several points in the Gospel key characters have the opportunity to dialogue with Jesus. In cases such as the Samaritan woman (4:4-42) and the man born blind (9:1-41), these conversations lead to conversion and new life. But others end in ambiguity (5:2-14; 3:1-10) or even a severing of ties with Jesus (6:66).

Pilate has the unique opportunity of talking face to face with Jesus at the moment of his Passion—a literary device that dominates John's narrative (18:33-19:12).[15] But tragically Pilate fails to recognize that he stands face to face with ultimate Truth (18:38) and ends up delivering Jesus to his enemies (19:16).

The most ferocious opponent of Jesus is offstage but fully active in the Johannine Passion story—Satan. The Gospel made that clear at the beginning of the Book of Glory when John notes that "the devil had already put it into the heart of Judas son of Simon Iscariot to betray (Jesus)" (13:2). Earlier, Jesus has told the disciples that one of them was a "devil" and the narrator tells the reader that Jesus was speaking of "Judas son of Simon Iscariot" (6:70-71). That demonic possession is consummated at the very moment Jesus hands Judas a morsel of bread at the meal, a sign of who was to betray him: "After he had received the piece of bread, Satan entered into him." (13:27). The reader is also aware that, in John's view, the leaders themselves in their symbolic role of rigid disbelief are also driven by Satan and, therefore, intent on Jesus' destruction. This was stated in the violent polemic of chapter 8 where Jesus accuses the leaders of having Satan as their parent: "You are from your father the devil, and you choose to do your father's desires. He was a murderer from the beginning and does not stand in the truth, because there is no truth in him." (8:44).

In the Johannine perspective, therefore, the opposition that leads to Jesus' Passion is not an alternate viewpoint carried to extremes nor simply a miscarriage of justice. Pulsating beneath

15 See above, pp. 68-71.

the opposition to Jesus is the very spirit of evil, attempting to thrwart God's work and to blunt the message of Jesus' redeeming word. That conviction fuels the uncompromising stance John gives both Jesus and his opposition in the Passion story and throughout the Gospel.

But John leaves no doubt that Jesus is triumphant over the power of evil, and the assertion of that is drenched in irony, an irony that stands at the heart of the Christian message. While evil instinctively attempts to kill Jesus and thereby destroy his power, the reader of the Gospel knows that in this very act of dying, a death for love, God's own power triumphs. Once again John's Gospel concentrates its dramatic force on the mysterious and paradoxical center of the Christian message: death leads to life—an assertion that overturns the power of darkness.

This judgment over the power of evil finds a particularly strong expression in one of the central symbols of the Johannine Passion story, that of "kingship." The dominance of the Roman trial scene in the Johannine narrative and the interface between Pilate, the representative of imperial power, and Jesus, the prisoner accused of claims to royalty, give this metaphor a crucial place in John's theology of the Passion.

Here, too, irony is a major Johannine literary tool.[16] The reader knows from the outset that Jesus *is* the royal Son of God, imbued with all power from on high. Even his enemies caught a glimpse of this awesome majesty at the moment of the arrest, when the very sound of his name drives them to the ground, powerless (18:6). And Pilate, too, even though drugged with disbelief, senses that the man he interrogates has a mysterious power and is fearful because of it (19:8).

But for most of the narrative, only irony provides the key to this scene. The trial's central issue is Jesus' supposed claim to kingship and, without introduction, Pilate poses that question: "Are you the King of the Jews?" (18:33). And Jesus himself will boldly declare his own claim: "You say that I am a king. For this I was born, and for this I came into the world . . ." (18:37).

But Jesus clearly teaches that his royal power is of a totally different nature than the brutalizing power familiar to Pilate and

---

[16] See above, pp. 68–98.

the Jewish leaders. His kingdom was not "from this world" (18:36). His royal power was not expressed, as Rome's and therefore Pilate's was, in dominating the Jews and in trading on a human life. And Pilate's own power was limited to what God would permit him (19:11). Jesus' royal mission was to come into the world "to testify to the truth" (18:37), the truth of God's love for the world ultimately expressed in Jesus' self-donation for his friends.

It is on this basis that irony drives a wedge between the symbols of power in which Pilate puts his stock and the totally different expression of power invested in Jesus. In an attempt to gain pity for Jesus, Pilate surrounds him with the symbols of imperial power: a crown; a purple cloak; homage by soldiers (19:1-3). Twice he leads Jesus outside his headquarters to the crowds in imitation of a ritual of public acclamation (19:4-5; 13-15). All of these symbols are deliberate mockeries: a thorn crown; homage that is a violent game; a royal procession that is meant to provoke pity and dismissal, not acclamation. In so doing, Pilate asserts that, in fact, Jesus is no king but a powerless and insignificant figure, one not worth a public condemnation. When expediency forces the procurator's hand and Jesus is executed, Pilate expresses his contempt for the Jewish leaders in continuing to mockingly assert the "royal status" of Jesus by fixing the placard to the cross, even though he and the leaders know that such is not the case (19:19-21).

In the end, all of the forces arrayed against Jesus are defeated. The opponents who believe that in turning Jesus over to execution they will be rid of him, only succeed in directing Jesus to that moment in which his tenacious love for his friends—the sign of God's love for the world—would be most forcefully demonstrated. John had already savored that irony in the words of Caiphas on the eve of the Passion: "You do not understand that it is better for you to have one man die for the people than to have the whole nation destroyed. He did not say this on his own, but being high priest that year he prophesied that Jesus was about to die for the nation, and not for the nation only, but to gather into one the dispersed children of God." (11:50-52). Satan who animated Judas finds that his machinations lead only to the defeat of death, not its triumph.

And one should not underestimate the political critique implicit in the Johannine treatment of the royal symbols.[17] The imperial power of Rome was not an anachronism when the Fourth Gospel was written. The representative power of a Roman procurator, the absolute authority claimed by the title "king" or "emperor," the fact of Rome's occupation of Palestine, the brutal sanction of crucifixion for any act of sedition—all of these give John's Passion story a dangerous edge in the world in which it was written. While John speaks of Jesus' kingship in "spiritual" tones— "My kingdom is not from this world" (18:36)—the reader knows that this does not mean that Jesus' authority has no impact on social and political realities nor that it was incapable of coming into radical conflict with existing political structures and imperial political claims.

John's Passion story shares with the other Gospels an implicit, yet unmistakable, critique of all political power that is animated by values other than that of the Gospel. The power of God which abided in Jesus and was given to the children of God who believed in him was far more powerful and would have far more transformative consequences than any political system.

That is demonstrated in the chasm that separates Pilate and Jesus in the Roman trial scene; the Roman governor cannot comprehend the nature of Jesus' authority nor does he realize the limits of his own. Jesus' authority was from God and was expressed in proclaiming the truth and in using every fiber of his being to express the love of God for the world. Self-transcendence, not self-aggrandizement, drove Jesus and was the ultimate expression of his divine power.

In the Passion story, the cross becomes the collision point between these two "worlds." To protect its interests and to assert its force, the power of Rome seized this Galilean and destroys his life through the grisly ritual of crucifixion. In so doing it expresses in public fashion its claim to ultimate power over life and death. In their blind opposition to Jesus, the religious leaders abandon the sure instinct of their faith. The biblical people knew well the limits of all human institutions and all claims to power other than that of God alone. The evangelist presses salt deep into

---

[17] On this point, see D. Rensberger, *Johannine Faith and Liberating Community,* esp. 87–106.

the wound by having the leaders acclaim: "We have no king but Caesar" (19:15).

But at the very moment that such oppressive power seems victorious it is denied its triumph. As death seeps in, Jesus acclaims "it is finished!"—his brand of power could reverse the torque of death and transform it into a rush of new life. In giving his life out of love, he was supremely free and fully alive. No human power, no oppressive machine could thwart the power of the cross.

JOHN'S PORTRAYAL OF THE JEWS

In the light of recent history, no reflection on John's Gospel can fail to add a footnote to this motif. By tending to merge the various groups of Jewish opponents to Jesus into one group, "the Jews," and by casting them as symbols of unbelief and aggressive hostility to Jesus, John's Gospel—perhaps more than any other—has unwittingly fueled Christian anti-semitism.[18]

"Unwittingly" is an accurate assessment of John's perspective. Two main reasons—one theological and the other historical—lead John to his negative portrayal of the Jewish leaders.[19] As we noted several times in the course of this study, John's theology tends to be "dualistic," that is, it casts its portrayal of Jesus and the response it demands in absolute terms. Jesus is the Incarnate Word, the Son of God, the last and complete revelation of God's love for the world, the Way and the Truth necessary for eternal life. On this level of discourse there is no room for other religious figures or means of salvation: the Temple, Moses and the Law, the Jewish liturgies—in John's perspective all are subsumed and replaced by the cosmic figure of Christ. And, therefore, response to Jesus must be on the same ultimate level: the

[18] On this issue, see the works of R. Fuller, "The 'Jews' in the Fourth Gospel," *Dialog* 16 (1977) 31-37; J. Leibig, "John and the Jews' Theological Antisemitism in the Fourth Gospel," *Journal of Ecumenical Studies* 20 (1983) 209-34; R. A. Culpepper, "The Gospel of John and the Jews," *Review and Expositor* 84 (1987) 273-88; D. Moody Smith, "Judaism and The Gospel of John," in J. Charlesworth (ed.), *Jews and Christians* (New York: Crossroad, 1990), 76-99.

[19] Although John uses a generic term, "Jews," it is clear in his Gospel that the group referred to is primarily the leaders, not the people as a whole; on this, see, U. C. von Walde, "The Johannine Jews: A Critical Survey," *New Testament Studies* 28 (1982) 33-60.

choice is to believe in Jesus, to choose the "light," to embrace "life"—or to disbelieve and thereby choose darkness and death.

In this world of clear choices, the opponents of Jesus could not be portrayed in anything other than absolute terms. From the traditions he received, the evangelist and his community knew that some of the leadership groups had undoubtedly been in conflict with Jesus on various points of law and had ultimately not accepted his message. This became the historical basis for the role they play in his theological and symbolic narrative.

Another historical factor may have led John to cast the Jewish leaders in sharply negative tones. The rift between early Christianity and rabbinic Judaism, a parting of the ways that was accelerated and complicated by the Roman suppression of the Jewish revolt in A.D. 70, undoubtedly had an influence on the Johannine community. We cannot be sure how fresh was the wound of this conflict between the early church and Judaism at the time John's Gospel took its final shape. But at some point in its history, the religious hostility experienced between Jews and Christians left its imprint on the perspective of the Gospel writer. The story of the man born blind whose parents fear expulsion from the synagogue because of association with Jesus seems to reflect this experience (9:22), as does the warning of Jesus at the last discourse: "They will put you out of the synagogues. Indeed, an hour is coming when those who kill you will think that by doing so they are offering worship to God." (16:2).[20]

Note that this was not a conflict between Gentiles on one side and Jews on another. Undoubtedly, many of the Johannine Christians were Jewish in origin and Jewish theology and symbols have a major influence on John's perspective. Therefore, this is not anti-semitism in the manner we speak of it today.

Nevertheless, John's portrayal of Jesus' opponents lends itself to anti-semitism when intepreters use the Gospel as a basis for hatred or contempt for Jews. This has been a tragic and even sacrilegious legacy. A Gospel whose core message is a proclamation of love should not be used in such a way that it drips hatred and prejudice into the lifeblood of the Church.

---

[20] See the analysis of this passage in J. L. Martyn, *History & Theology in the Fourth Gospel* (Nashville: Abingdon, rev. ed., 1979), 24–36.

Some have suggested that the only antidote to this problem is to alter the text of John's Gospel either by translating the term "Jews" as "Judeans," thereby making the term less generic and more historically circumscribed, or, at least for liturigical services, to edit John's text all together so that offense passages are not proclaimed in Christian churches.

None of these solutions is completely satisfying and perhaps no solution based on altering the text can be. A more difficult but ultimately more substantial solution is to awaken readers, listeners and preachers of the Gospel of John to its historical circumstances and to the full meaning of its theology, thereby enabling Christian proclamation to attack anti-Semitism, not feed it.

The death of Jesus has redemptive value and from the Crucified Jesus new life streams into the World.

Implicit in all of the themes we have thus far considered is the Johannine conviction—one shared with the Synoptic Gospels—that the death of Jesus has transforming power. John, of course, views the death in unbreakable connection with the resurrection of Jesus—his return to the Father in glory, as Johannine language would express it. But the very moment of death itself unleashes redemptive power and effects human salvation.

The portrayal of Jesus as the revealer of God, for example, means that those who come to "understand" or "know" or "see" who God is through the love sign of Jesus' selfless death for the world are empowered to become new beings themselves, to be "reborn" as children of God. Obviously, the categories of "knowing," "understanding," "seeing" and "believing" as used in Johannine theology are not solely intellectual exercises or mere acts of perception. In the Johannine world—one influenced by Greek and Jewish culture—to "know" someone, to "understand" God's Word, meant that one's whole being was transformed.

Therefore, the revelation of God's love for the world expressed through the crucifixion of Jesus bore overwhelming power of transformation. Those who understood the meaning of Jesus' death would have the entire horizon of their being—mind, heart, will—changed by an awareness of God's truth. The testimony of the witness which concludes the death scene reflects an awareness of the power this sign effects: "He who saw this has testified so that you also may believe. His testimony is true, and he knows that he tells the truth." (19:35).

Other events and motifs of the Passion story reinforce John's proclamation of the redemptive power of Jesus' death. As we will discuss in more detail below, the presentation of the mother of Jesus to the Beloved Disciple may imply for John that the Christian community itself is born at the moment of Jesus' death (see 19:26-27). The haunting signs of water and blood that spring from the lanced side of the crucified Jesus are also indications of the redemptive power of the cross (19:32-37). From the body of the crucified Jesus, the new temple of God (2:21), flows the power of the Spirit into the world, a spirit symbolized in life-giving water and nourishing blood.

And, finally, John's deft use of Passover symbolism also helps proclaim the power of Jesus' death.[21] Jesus the "lamb of God" (1:29, 36) encounters death at the very moment the Passover lambs are slain in the temple (19:14). And Jesus's legs are spared fracture as the Passover lamb must, aligning his death with the Scriptures (19:33, 36). Thereby John associates the death of Jesus with the feast and ritual of Passover, that primal Jewish feast that celebrated the liberating power of the exodus. Exodus was the model redemptive act, bringing Israel from death to life. The Passover meal celebrated that inaugural redemption of Israel and looked forward to God's final deliverance.[22] John implies that Jesus himself embodies that redemptive action of God and in laying down his life he would mark the believer with the liberating sign of Passover.

In typical Johannine fashion, all of these are enticing "signs" not explicit propositions. Cumulatively they portray the moment of Jesus' death as a moment of incredible transformation, one in which new life leaps into being. The pain of Jesus' death is not terminal pain but a birth pang and when new life appears, even that pain is turned into joy (16:20-21).

Despite the subtlety of these symbols, the redemptive interpretation of Jesus' death is not a risk. On more than one occasion

---

[21] See above, pp. 33–34.

[22] See A. Saldarini, *Jesus and Passover* (New York: Paulist, 1984), esp. 71–79.

as the Gospel drama had unfolded, the Johannine Jesus had clearly proclaimed with multiple images that his death was a redemptive death: his flesh was given "for the life of the world" (6:51); as a Good Shepherd he would lay down his life for the sheep in order that they might have "eternal life" (10:15, 28); as a grain of wheat dying in the earth he would bear much fruit (12:24); and at the last supper he promised that when he had "departed" he would send the Paraclete to them (16:7). The triumphant mood of the Johannine Passion and its enticing symbols of new life emerging at the cross must be read in the light of the Gospel as a whole.

II. The Passion and John's Portrayal of the Life of Faith

Throughout the Johannine Passion narrative, as in the entire Gospel, the figure of Jesus commands the attention of the reader. But the illumination of John's Christology also falls on other characters in the narrative, particularly in their varying responses to Jesus and his mission. Their roles help define the Johannine understanding of the life of faith. The crisis point of suffering and death becomes a public stage on which the struggle of faith and the meaning of Christian life stand out in sharp relief.

The crisis of the Passion reveals the meaning of faith and the cost of discipleship.

The opponents of Jesus illustrate the tragedy of unbelief. Their refusal to believe in Jesus leads them to ally themselves with the Roman ruler and ultimately to betray their own allegiance to God's sovereignty when they declare: "we have no king but Caesar!" (19:15).

Judas the apostate disciple also meets a fate that corresponds to his betrayal. Unlike Matthew or Luke, John does not narrate the death of Judas but the reader knows that this disciple reaps the rewards of evil and is "lost" (17:12).

Pilate's fate, too, is not projected in the narrative but the reader observes the tragic moment when this man literally misses the opportunity of a lifetime as God's Truth stands before him and yet he fails to grasp who Jesus is or what is his origin (18:38; 19:9).

It falls to another group of characters, few in number but eloquent in testimony, to exemplify the more positive response of nascent faith. Similar to the Synoptic versions, John's Passion story is not studded with heroic examples other than that of Jesus himself. The Mother of Jesus and the Beloved Disciple remain near the cross but they have mostly a passive role, a faithful presence as Jesus encounters death and the recipients of his final words of care (19:26-27). The eyewitness testimony of presumably this same Beloved Disciple is underscored as the scene concludes (19:35).[23] Along with them are Mary the wife of Clophas and Mary Magdalene (19:25). We learn nothing more of them in the Passion story itself, but Mary Magdalene's faith will erupt in the resurrection appearance stories of chapter 20.[24]

There are three other characters who take a more active role in the Passion drama and offer more content to John's portrayal of faith. Peter is the prime example. Peter reacts aggressively at the moment of the arrest when he lashes out at the high priest's slave (18:10). With the assistance of "another disciple" Peter also gains entry into the courtyard of the High Priest, only to be confronted by the woman who was the porter and in the glare of her questions, to tragically deny his association with Jesus (18:15-18; 25-27). After this Peter has no more role in the Passion story itself, returning to the Gospel drama with the discovery of the empty tomb (20:1-10) and his encounter with the Risen Christ in Galilee (chapter 21).[25]

Both of these incidents in the Passion portray Peter in a negative light. At first blush his attempt to protect Jesus at the moment of the arrest might seem an act of loyalty, but that judgment must be tempered by the negative reaction of Jesus himself. Peter's use of the sword reveals how little he understands Jesus. Jesus rebukes Peter and tells him to put his sword back in its sheath (18:11). As Jesus bluntly tells Pilate, only if Jesus' kingdom were animated by the false and brutal values of "this world" would his followers be encouraged to take up the sword (18:36).

---

[23] Probably the same disciple leads Peter into the courtyard of the high priest; see the discussion of 18:15-16, above, pp. 63–64.

[24] See above, p. 137.

[25] See above, pp. 134–43.

And Peter's painful denial of Jesus is also a lesson in the breakdown of discipleship. Despite the warnings Jesus had given him and Peter's own confident assessment of his endurance (13:37-38), Simon Peter succumbs to fear and three times publicly denies that he is one of Jesus' disciples (18:17, 25, 27).

Coupled with John's admiration for the Beloved Disciple throughout the Gospel, one could be tempted to conclude that the Fourth Gospel is thoroughly negative about the figure of Peter.[26] At almost every turn, the Beloved Disciple is more responsive to Jesus and more consistent in his understanding and faith.[27]

But John's preference for the Beloved Disciple as the exemplar of discipleship and the grounding point for the tradition of the Fourth Gospel does not lead to a completely negative portrayal of Peter. John, in fact, uses the figure of Peter to portray the struggles of discipleship. There is no question about the authenticity of Simon's vocation to be a disciple, even if in John's account he is not the first to be called (1:40-42).[28] And Peter will play more than a minor role in the Gospel itself. His response in chapter six is surely seen by the Gospel as an example of authentic faith, coming as it does in contrast to those who were turning away from Jesus: "Lord, to whom can we go? You have the words of eternal life. We have come to believe and know that you are the Holy One of God." (6:68-69). At other times, such as his initial refusal to have his feet washed (13:6-11) or in his bravado when he vows to follow Jesus to death (13:36-38), Simon appears impulsive and uncomprehending but never hostile to Jesus.

The full portrayal of Peter in John's Gospel must take into account chapters 20 and 21. As we noted above, the Fourth Gospel

---

[26] See, for example, A. Droge, "The Status of Peter in the Fourth Gospel: John 18:10-11," *Journal of Biblical Literature* 109 (1990) 307-11; he concludes that Peter's taking up the sword in the garden is further evidence that the disciple belongs to those who do not comprehend the nature of Jesus' kingdom and therefore "has come dangerously close to being placed beyond the Johannine pale." (311).

[27] See above, pp. 136, 141-43.

[28] In the Synoptics Peter is first called; not so in John. Note, too, that instead of a "call story" we have the characteristic Johannine device in which disciples are drawn to Jesus either by direct contact (1:35-39, 43) or through an intermediary (1:40-42; 45-47). Contrary to Droge, this is not a negative device but may be a model for the transmission of faith within the experience of the Johannine community itself.

rehabilitates the figure of Peter in these chapters.[29] Resurrection faith dawns slowly for Peter but the dawn does come. And in chapter 21, Jesus deliberately reconciles Peter's threefold denial and gives him a missionary and pastoral responsibility for the community. Some authors believe that these episodes, particularly ch. 21 are attempts to offset the negative portrayal of Peter in the body of the Gospel. While this might be the case, even in the body of the Gospel Peter is not portrayed in purely negative tones, and, in any case, we are choosing to work with the portrayal that now stands in the fully redacted form of the Gospel, not its hypothetical earlier stage. In its present form, the figure of Peter stands not as an example of failed faith, but of the travails discipleship can experience, of the impact of human weakness, and of the triumph of grace.

This is precisely what the crisis of the Passion provokes. In this storm center of opposition to Jesus, the disciples can clearly see the cost of following him. The "hatred" of the world for Jesus spills over on the disciples. This is what Jesus had warned them at the last supper:

> "If the world hates you, be aware that it hated me before it hated you. If you belonged to the world, the world would love you as its own. Because you do not belong to the world, but I have chosen you out of the world—therefore the world hates you. Remember the word that I said to you, 'Servants' are not greater than their master. If they persecuted me, they will persecute you . . . But they will do all these things to you on account of my name, because they do not know him who sent me." (15:18-21).

Peter had declared his intent of following Jesus even to death but he had underestimated the power of fear, and when confronted with the risk of exposure as a disciple, he had chosen to deny his very identity. Only the reconciling grace of the Risen Christ and the power of the Paraclete would help the disciples withstand the withering fire of persecution and enmity and enable them to give fearless testimony before the world. "In the

[29] See above, pp. 142–43.

world you face persecution. But take courage; I have conquered the world!'' (16:33).

Thus the Gospel's portrayal of Peter, while not always flattering, is ultimately compassionate. Peter is not counted among those "lost"—only Judas fills that terrible category. Jesus would not allow Peter to be "snatched from his hand" (10:29) and that, the Gospel suggests, is the ultimate strength of all discipleship under duress. Not only would Peter be redeemed and reconciled with the Risen Christ, but he would be entrusted with apostolic authority and restored to his mission.

Two other characters are dressed in somewhat ambiguous tones in John's Passion story. We know little about Joseph of Arimathea except that he was a "secret" disciple of Jesus out of fear of reprisal from the Jews (19:38). Nicodemus who appears at several points in the Gospel is another figure in the Gospel whose faith seems less than exemplary.[30] But the same standard applied to Peter might be applied to these two figures, that they be judged by the full span of their Gospel roles. Whatever their previous weakness may have been, their willingness to risk public exposure in claiming the crucified body of Jesus and their lavish homage offered to him in the burial ritual suggests they have shed their fear. In contrast to Peter, the trauma of suffering and death have emboldened these two disciples, drawing from them the courage of witness that previously they could not summon.

There is a realism in the cast of characters John places in the Passion drama. The opportunity for power displays the terrible choices of his opponents and the empty values of Pilate. For some, such as Peter, the trial of suffering and persecution is overwhelming, exposing an immature discipleship. For others the shock of Jesus' death helps them shed their hesitations and come out into the light, exemplifying the magnetic force of the cross predicted by Jesus: "And I, when I am lifted up from the earth, will draw all people to myself." (12:32). The cross stands at the center of John's perspective—source of both judgment and new life.

---

[30] See above, pp. 130–33.

The cross of Jesus gives new meaning to the Christian encounter with death.

The triumphant character of John's Passion narrative does not leave it without significance for the Christian experience of death. Each of the Gospels has a distinct approach in portraying Jesus' death and from each of them can be drawn some reflections on the experience of suffering and death.

First of all, John's Passion story asserts what is a basic conviction of the entire New Testament: the death and resurrection of Jesus have robbed death of its sting. Eternal life, not death, have the last word: that is a message trumpeted on practically every page of John's Passion story. Death for Jesus becomes the hour of "glory" because it is the moment in which his mission is completed and he returns to his Father. Implicitly, Johannine theology sees in Jesus' destiny the future of all believers. That link was stated in the final testament of Jesus. Jesus is the forerunner of the Christian: "Where I am going, you cannot follow me now, but you will follow afterward." (13:36). The bond forged between Jesus and his disciples, between the vine and the branches, could not be severed by death.

Other images reinforce this conviction of victory over death and add to the paradoxical luster of John's Passion account. In the last discourse, Jesus had spoken of death as a "return" home, as a "going" to his father (see 14:1-4, 12, 28-29; 16:5-7, 28; 17:11, 13). Corresponding to this is Jesus' promise not to leave the disciples as "orphans" but that he would first send the Paraclete to be with them and ultimately return to take them "home" with him (see 14:3, 18-19, 28; 16:7, 16; 17:24).

These evocative images of homecoming, of reunion, and final rest ransack the terror of death and explain why John presents the Passion of Jesus—so terrifying in its surface reality—as, in fact, a story of triumph in which Jesus acts with serenity and confidence. Faith enables the Christian to see death not as a termination of life nor even as entry into estrangement, but as a return home to God in the company of the Risen Christ. Probably without knowing its immediate source, generation after generation of Christian has faced death with peace on the basis of these Gospel images and the faith they express.[31]

The manner of Jesus' death described in John's Passion story not only expresses a sense of peace and completion—"It is finished" (19:30)—expressive of his return to God, but also a confidence and sense of purpose that coincides with the mood of martyrdom. Jesus faces his captors without hesitation and is, indeed, in command of the situation even though he is the prisoner. He confronts interrogators and takes up his own cross. There is no lament, no hint of travail. He completes his work and dies— slaking his thirst for God's will by freely accepting his death.

A key text we have noted several times in our study of John's Passion is to the point here as well: "For this reason the Father loves me, because I lay down my life in order to take it up again. No one takes it from me, but I lay it down of my own accord. I have power to take it up again. I have received this command from my Father." (10:17-18). Undoubtedly, this majestic freedom reflects John's view of the identity of Jesus. As the Incarnate Son of God Jesus is not subject to the agents of history. He freely lays down his life and freely takes it up again in his pursuit of the mission entrusted to him by his Father.

At first glance, a perspective such as this has little relevance for the Christian experience of death. Surely no one, no matter how heroic, can be confident of such command over their destiny. But further reflection may tell a different story. The Jesus who expresses such confidence and power is the very Jesus who, on one level of the Passion story, is in fact a prisoner: arrested by soldiers, subject to interrogation and torture, condemned to death, and publicly executed with his limp body violated by a lance to insure his death. But despite these brutalities, the reader of the Gospel senses that Jesus is, indeed, supremely free—more free than his captors who believe they hold his life in the balance.

Christian experience throughout centuries of persecution witnesses to similar Passion stories. Even as brutal force threatens human life, people of faith can exercise complete freedom: willingly sacrificing their lives for the sake of the Gospel; refusing to render violence for violence, refusing to base their lives on the

---

[31] One thinks, for example, of the now famous quotation of John XXIII shortly before his death: "My bags are packed and I am ready to go." The words have a "Johannine" flavor.

false values of their captors. No power on earth, even demonic power, can rob the Christian of this freedom and this triumph.

In its own way, the Johannine Passion narrative is a primer on Christian witness and the vocation of martyrdom.

Author Index

Subject Index

Scripture Index